Questions from the Pews

Questions from the Pews

Theological Narratives in Reply

S. P. KING

WIPF & STOCK · Eugene, Oregon

QUESTIONS FROM THE PEWS
Theological Narratives in Reply

Wipf & Stock
An Imprint of Wipf and Stock Publishers
199 W. 8th Ave., Suite 3
Eugene, OR 97401

www.wipfandstock.com

PAPERBACK ISBN: 978-1-5326-7545-4
HARDCOVER ISBN: 978-1-5326-7546-1
EBOOK ISBN: 978-1-5326-7547-8

Manufactured in the U.S.A.   10/29/19

I dedicate this book to Warren, my loving, patient, kind,
inspiring, supportive, dependable,
charming, and most wonderful husband
who read every word of this book
and thinks I use too many adjectives.

Contents

Preface

THIS BOOK IS AN invitation to question and clarify what you believe about the Christian faith. It came about as a result of questions that were repeatedly presented to me during my pastoral ministry. These questions arose from people who valued critical thinking and intellectual integrity and wanted to think things through, rather than merely accept long-standing dictums. They did not want simplistic clichés, but substantial and tangible information through authentic conversation.

I was intrigued to find that the questions are the same for the faithful who are seeking a deeper understanding as they are for non-Christians who want to learn more about what Christians believe. Therefore, although this book concerns the Christian faith, it is not a book solely for Christians. It is a tool to explore the faith in an environment that is devoid of efforts to indoctrinate. The issues discussed in this book are not presented with an intention to sway your faith in a particular direction, but rather to serve as a framework in which you can objectively examine your beliefs.

Each chapter of the book focuses on a recurrent question that deserves more attention than can be given with a handshake at the door after a worship service. The following questions are representative of those deliberated. What is the origin of the Bible? Why does God allow suffering? What does it mean *to be saved*? Why are there so many denominations? Do other faiths contain truth? Although there are libraries filled with volumes of books dedicated to each question, not everyone has the time to delve into every issue with days or weeks of research. The purpose of this book is to deliver a thorough but accessible summary of current scholarship on each topic. While some of the questions have definitive answers, others elude a conclusive or absolute response. The chapter titles are largely self-explanatory and although each chapter is capable of being a stand-alone resource, I have tried to order them such that there is a logical progression through the book. The chapters proceed from background information about Christianity to how the faith applies to daily life. If you wish to immediately go to the chapters that most interest you, the only suggestion I make is to read the chapter on salvation prior to any that follow, as some of the later chapters draw on its material.

Three approaches are implemented to address the topics in each chapter. The book firstly employs an academic or scientific approach, to the extent possible. Such an approach utilizes known facts, as well as historical evidence. However, science and logic rarely completely satisfy questions of faith. Another approach, more abstract, considers the spiritual aspects of the topic. This approach is less easily defined but is comparable to the appreciation of music. While music can be studied in terms of physics and acoustics, we must also recognize the esoteric effects it has on the listener. The spiritual attribute of the Christian faith, while difficult to elucidate, cannot be dismissed, for it is often the means through which we receive divine inspiration. The book also approaches the topics from a biblical perspective, for no discussion of the Christian faith would be complete without letting the text of the Bible speak. The biblical exploration will strive to keep the entire context of the Bible in view.

While the book is intended for a wide audience, and I believe objectivity is of paramount importance, I readily acknowledge that it is impossible to completely divorce my experiences, theological understandings, and North American worldview from my writing. Moreover, I realize that readers of the book will have their own unique viewpoint. My worldview is influenced by the path my life has taken, which includes pastoring in a mainline Christian denomination, chaplaincy experience in a major trauma hospital, a master of divinity degree from Fuller Theological Seminary, eighteen years of corporate experience as a computer programmer, and a bachelor of science degree in education, with teaching fields of mathematics and physical education. In addition, my husband, Warren, and I lived for more than two years in the Middle East in a country with a predominantly Muslim population, where we enjoyed unique opportunities for cross-cultural experiences and faith formation.

I have been fortunate to enjoy many wonderful companions throughout my faith formation. I would like to specifically thank the Rev. Gilbert H. Vieira for his steadfast friendship and counsel in my journey over the last thirty-five years. The constancy of his faith and the depth of his wisdom have been invaluable to my husband and me. We also benefitted from the friendship and guidance of the late Rev. Jerry A. Zandstra during our formative experience in the Middle East. Jerry was a beacon in the literal and figurative desert of my spiritual life. Upon returning to America, I attended Fuller Theological Seminary, where I enjoyed instruction from a distinguished body of professors who were preeminent in their field. I would particularly like to recognize Arthur G. Patzia, professor emeritus of New Testament, for his unwavering dedication to the faith and his students. Each of these persons has had a part in my understanding of the faith, and I am grateful for their walking alongside me.

In the exploration of one's beliefs, it is helpful to have sincere and faithful companions. I hope this book can serve that purpose and contribute to your study of the Christian faith. For those who wish to more deeply pursue a specific topic of interest, I have provided an appendix with reputable references for each chapter. Indeed, I hope that the appendix and bibliography will be useful aspects of the book. Reading this book may lead to a little mental exertion, especially if it leads you to examine views that conflict with your own. There may even be times when we must agree to disagree, but I hope that by the end of your studies you will be at peace with what you believe and know why you believe it.

1

Belief: Does It Make Any Difference?

BELIEFS GENERALLY HAVE A vague beginning and are developed over time as a product of our undaunted curiosity. The persistent "why" questions of curious children begin a lifelong process of developing and expanding their belief system. What were some of the first things you wondered about? What do you wonder about now?

Our beliefs include but are not limited to theological convictions. Addressing non-religious beliefs as well as those that relate to Christianity seems an appropriate way to proceed. I can recall a moment of wondering when, as a child in 1964, I yearned for a deeper understanding. I was in a Sunday school class and had dutifully made the prescribed paper ornament to hang on the Christmas tree. The night before, my mother had curled my hair and pressed my white blouse and pretty red Christmas jumper that she had sewn and decorated with sequins. We had been alerted that flash bulbs would be popping, as a crew was being sent to document this class for the church's Christmas publication. As I hung my ornament on the tree, I was somehow aware that this was the perfect picture the photographers wanted, so I held the pose. However, I was also aware that the picture would fail to capture the questions that lay hidden behind this facade of activity.

My innermost thoughts, which I remember to this day, were "Please, someone tell me the real Christmas message. I know there is more." I left that classroom sad and disheartened, somehow knowing that the Christmas, which was extensively celebrated by those who filled my small world, was not to be found in the paper ornaments on that tree. That picture resurfaced decades later as we sifted through my father's belongings and is reproduced here. In my early life, after Sunday school, my father would occasionally take my sisters and I to the drug store where we would sit at the counter on the rotating stools and twirl and talk and drink a cherry cola. Perhaps I told him of my yearnings that day—I don't remember. However, I now realize my theological belief system took a large leap that day, not in the form of answers, but in the form of questions. Curiosity precedes belief.

We all hold beliefs. Even an atheist has a theological belief: believing there is no God. An agnostic believes that we are unable to know if there is a God, and thus suspends judgment one way or the other. The Christian is a theist, believing in one all-powerful, all-knowing, completely good God that created the universe. Many people have plunged into study and reflection and have developed a clear picture of what they believe to be true. Others may not have gained enough clarity about their beliefs to state them. Some adopt the beliefs of their ancestors and call them their own. Some even claim to have no beliefs, which is itself a belief.

Our beliefs make a difference, for they are at the very heart of who we are and ultimately guide our actions. If we are unsure of our beliefs, we can catch a glimpse from the mosaic formed by our collection of tweets, texts, Facebook pages, and other social media. Beliefs shape our lives and influence every choice we make. Philosophers have stated that "the ideas one really believes largely determine the kind of person one becomes."[1] Every choice, from what toothpaste we buy to the political candidates we support, is a confession of our beliefs. We confess our beliefs every day with

1. Moreland and Craig, *Philosophical Foundations*, 11.

our purchases, the words we say and write, and by every lifestyle choice we make. What we believe is who we are.

Our life may become fragmented when we do not have a good grasp on our beliefs. Lacking firm clarity may cause us to be easily swayed when our beliefs are challenged, or when our beliefs jeopardize the fulfillment of our desires. Each of us may not have done the work to understand what we believe, but we can be sure that marketing firms, political campaigns, and advertising agencies have. What we give our time, money, words, votes, and ultimately our hearts to can be traced back to our beliefs.

Do our beliefs matter? I believe they do, and it benefits each of us greatly to examine them. It is important to have clarity and consistency in what we hold true. We innately hunger for truths that we can believe in and which will steady us in uncertain times. Such truth can be elusive, and affronts to our beliefs may result in elements of doubt which can linger and hover close by. But when we are clear on our beliefs, we are free to acknowledge alternate views without compromising our own values or inflicting ungracious judgment on others. Still, it benefits us to have our assumptions challenged, because, ironically, it is only by constantly questioning our beliefs that we can both affirm them and be open to fresh insights.

How Do We Acquire Our Beliefs?

We cannot believe something just because we are told to. Nor can we believe something simply because we want to. Suppose you wanted to believe that the sun rises in the west. No matter how hard you tried, you could not believe this. The overwhelming evidence from our observations gives us confidence that the sun rises in the east.

We justify our beliefs by collecting data with our own eyes. It is human nature to pursue all trains of thought. We investigate all sources at our disposal and evaluate these sources for trustworthiness. We form our beliefs after deliberating over information and theories and then merging in our own experiences and intuitions. However, for some of the beliefs we hold, absolute certainty remains elusive or impractical to prove. We frequently do not have enough data to completely verify a belief. Have we observed every single sunrise? No, but we go ahead and trust that belief because it fits within our current awareness. We will hold on to a belief that is consistent with our knowledge and experiences until new evidence appears that causes us to question it. Questioning a belief can be a good thing, and often leads us down a new avenue of thought.

Challenges to Our Beliefs

An event that creates an inconsistency in our current beliefs presents us with an opportunity to search for new evidence. This anomaly may be anything from additional scientific data, a unique problem that eludes a solution, a recently exposed awareness of some issue in the world around us, or the result of a fresh personal experience. We are free to acknowledge the anomaly or not. We are free to choose what beliefs we explore and free to choose our evidence. But to increase the odds that we will discover a truth worthy of acquiring, we must not knowingly ignore inconsistencies or exclude evidence.

The human mind is very complex, and it can furiously hold on to untruths when protecting a worldview or protecting some aspect of one's way of life. Consciously or subconsciously, fear can be induced when our beliefs are brought into question. This unease can make us feel like we have been pushed to the edge of a cliff, and the desire to move back toward safer ground causes us to tenaciously grasp our current beliefs. We are uncomfortable when we have been destabilized. It can simply be easier to hold on to an untruth than to reverse a deeply held conviction. The only alternative to holding firm is to do the hard work of exploring the new evidence. Unshakable beliefs which are held contrary to overwhelming evidence can be experienced at a personal level or played out in view of the entire world by a large group.

We might think we are immune from such folly. But be careful, for it can and has happened insidiously to some of the greatest minds right out in the open for all to see. I will illustrate this point by tracing the highlights of a historic struggle in which new scientific evidence was not only ignored but suppressed in order to preserve the status quo.

Cautionary Tale

In AD 150 Ptolemy described our solar system in detail but erroneously placed the earth at the center and described the sun and planets revolving around the earth. This geocentric model became a truth held by the scientific community. The religious authorities also supported and promoted this model. At first there was no reason to doubt it—the scientists maintained it and it was congruent with the religious authority's interpretation of scriptures. In the Bible, Joshua 10:12–13 speaks of the sun being ordered to stop its normal movement and stand still. This passage was incorrectly interpreted as implying that the normal order was for the sun to revolve around the earth. Other references are in the poetic genera of the Psalms. Psalm 93:1b states "He [the Lord] has established the world; it shall never be moved." Psalm 104:5 reads "You [the Lord] set the earth on its foundations, so that it shall never be shaken." These verses were used by the religious authorities to validate the idea that the earth was at the center of the solar system and the other bodies revolve around the earth. For centuries, there was no reason to question this belief, so it stood accepted.

But then almost fourteen hundred years after Ptolemy's model was established, Nicolaus Copernicus observed a glitch. He was perplexed by his observation that some planets apparently moved backwards and planets farther from the sun moved slower. To account for these observations he located the sun, not the earth, at the center, and with that redress, the heliocentric model was born. Copernicus explained, "Only in this way [placing the sun at the center], do we find a sure harmonious connection."[2] Satisfied with this model, Copernicus published his findings in *On the Revolutions of the Heavenly Bodies* in 1543, just before his death. However, his death left the heliocentric model without a champion, and it was not given much attention until 1609 when Galileo Galilei turned to the heavens with a new instrument, the telescope. His astronomical observations brought more evidence and validity to the heliocentric model.

But not all were ready for this discovery. Tenaciously holding to the old geocentric model, with the earth at the center of our solar system, was the Roman Catholic Church. Changing their belief about the order of the solar system would cause two problems for them. First, they would have to change their interpretation of scripture, and second, they would have to accept that an interpretation of scripture outside of their authority was more valid than their own. For it was Galileo, who was not authorized by the church to interpret scripture, who provided a new interpretation.

Galileo proposed that these scripture passages, traditionally interpreted from a literal standpoint, could just as well be interpreted as allegory. However, Galileo was up against the brewing of a perfect storm. The Protestant Reformation was in full swing. The Reformation challenged the church's claim that they alone could interpret scripture. This situation created added tension, making the church unwilling to give away any authority of biblical interpretation to Galileo. The evidence from the scientific community continued to grow, but nothing could convince the Roman Catholic Church to reverse its grip on the geocentric model. In this atmosphere, Galileo was brought before the Inquisition and was convicted of heresy for promoting the heliocentric model which contradicted the current interpretation of the

2. Couper and Henbest, *History of Astronomy*, 98.

scriptures. He was forced to recant and was placed under house arrest for the remainder of his years.[3]

Galileo continued to gather evidence in favor of the heliocentric model, but even after his death the church still held tenaciously to their erroneous belief. Texts which promoted heliocentrism were put on the Catholic Church's *Index of Prohibited Books*. It was not until 1758 that the general prohibition of these texts was lifted. But prohibition remained for Copernicus's *On the Revolutions of the Heavenly Bodies* and Galileo's *Dialogue Concerning the Two Chief World Systems* until 1835, even though in 1820 the Catholic Church finally accepted that the earth moves around the sun. And even more amazing, it was not until 1992 that Pope John Paul II formally recognized the error of Galileo's judges.[4]

This irrational astronomical and church history controversy may seem ridiculous to most of us today, but the events during those 450 years demonstrate just how powerfully and to what extent one can go in order to protect a strongly held belief that, if proven untrue, would cause one to modify the precepts one lives by. Passages in the Bible that imply the earth does not move, thus placing it at the center of our solar system, are now commonly interpreted as if the writer is taking an *allegorical* geocentric view, much like we would do if viewing the stars from our backyard. At that moment we are at a point standing still and looking out upon the planets and stars which appear to move.

Theology is not the same order of discourse as science. It would be risky to let our faith depend on a strictly literal interpretation of scripture. It would be just as risky to fear that science will conflict with scripture and unravel one's beliefs. A sturdy faith need not fear intellectual honesty. Even at the start of this controversy in the 1500s, some in the Roman Catholic Church recognized that we occasionally ask scripture to answer questions it was not intended to answer. During the beginning of this geocentric/heliocentric controversy a Vatican librarian is quoted as saying, "The Bible is a book about how one goes to Heaven—not how Heaven goes."[5]

The fact that the controversy involved discourse between church authorities and scientists gave rise to additional scrutiny and attention, for in those days, theologians and scientists often operated under the same umbrella. Over time scientific discourse has slowly separated from church authority, but a complete break is unlikely because ethical dilemmas keep the two intertwined. There are many medical and technological advances

3. Cross and Livingstone, *Oxford Dictionary Christian Church*, 651.

4. Cross and Livingstone, *Oxford Dictionary Christian Church*, 651.

5. Couper and Henbest, *History of Astronomy*, 146.

that were unimaginable at the time the scriptures were penned, but many still look to the scriptures to inform an ethical response to emerging technologies. Our beliefs are, and most likely always will be, under constant evaluation in a search for truth.

This astronomical controversy has been a glaring example of holding a belief in error. The inclusion of this example is *not* to instill any ill will toward the Roman Catholic Church. They do not in any way have a monopoly on denial of evidence. The purpose of including this controversy is simply to caution us and to encourage us to approach our belief system with our eyes wide open, to consider evidence from many disciplines, and to recognize that our beliefs have real consequences in our lives as well as consequences in the lives of those around us.

Discovering Truth

So how do we approach building our belief system and steer clear of error? How do we continuously move in the direction of truth? We hold beliefs in many disciplines: scientific, economic, educational, legal, medical, and political to name a few. However, if there is one system that informs and undergirds our decisions in all the other theaters, it is our theological belief system; for it advises and informs our ethical and moral responses in the other areas of our lives. Our world has become more diverse, and we are now exposed to many world religions in our daily lives (I will address this plurality in chapter 11). But for now, I will concentrate on how we might discover truth when building Christian theological beliefs.

In surveying the works of theologians that have made positive contributions to understanding the Christian faith, some common characteristics stand out. These searchers of truth adopt approaches that are both unsentimental and practical. Their investigations are more than symbolic feel-good attempts to confirm long held traditions or reaffirmations of the simplified accounts we tell children. Nor do their approaches attempt to force a conclusion. Their approach is open-minded and unbiased, allowing them to consider ideas that are outside of their personal conclave. In such an atmosphere, there is a good chance that one's efforts will be rewarded with truth.

Theologian John Wesley (1703–91) approached his exploration of the Christian faith with a practical and unassuming framework similar to that just described. His life and work are well documented, and his methods have been studied and posthumously labeled the Wesleyan Quadrilateral. The fundamental components of this Quadrilateral are a good place for us to begin. Simply stated, the four resources that are identified in Wesley's process of discovering truth are scripture, tradition, reason and experience.[6] I will expound on each of these shortly. But I think the Quadrilateral stops short of a very important element in Wesley's and many others' faith development, and that element is revelation. While revelation can be elusive or hard to define, Wesley himself declared that a turning point in his life of faith was when he felt his heart strangely warmed.[7] At that moment of revelation, Wesley's doubt of his standing with Christ was erased. He had received assurance of his faith. He spent much reflection on what this revelation meant and how it came about. Wesley even suffered detractors who questioned the authenticity of his revelation. Episodes similar to this strange warming of the heart have been observed by many students of the scriptures. These encounters are very powerful and personal and deserve to be considered as a fifth source in a search for truth. They are not experiences that can be explained by logical arguments, but rather moments which provoke an overwhelming feeling that whatever the revelation is, it is from God, and it often supplants a troubled heart with a sense of peace.

Returning to the first element, scripture, we examine the role of the Bible. This book is shared by Christians the world over as the primary source for what Christians believe. How this particular set of writings came to be the primary source of the Christian faith will be discussed more fully in chapter 2. But it cannot be denied that against great odds, this unique collection of literature has been preserved over millennia.

It is not always an easy text to read. There is not a similar genre of literature that prepares us to know how to approach it. However, the indisputable way to fail to obtain the truths that the Bible reveals is simply to not read it. So for now, I would simply implore that the words of the Bible be included when discerning truths of the Christian faith, for Christians share the belief that God addresses each and every person within the pages of this unique book and invites them to respond.

While the scriptures are the primary source for elucidating the Christian faith, much can also be learned from the writings and traditions of early Christian witnesses. Such sources can take the form of early church documents, creeds, and the research and reforms of centuries of theologians. Today's Christians can stand on the shoulders of those before them as we continue to broaden our understandings. However, tradition alone does not guarantee truth. The cautionary tale concerning astronomy and Galileo

6. Maddox, *Responsible Grace*, 36.

7. Heitzenrater, *Mirror and Memory*, 106–7.

warns us that there is more to finding truth than just adhering to the tradition of earlier Christian witnesses.

In addition to the collective experiences that contributed to traditions, personal experiences are also part of informing and developing a belief system. Individually, we cannot separate an understanding of the Christian faith apart from our experiences. If we take the time to compare and contrast our experiences alongside Christian beliefs, then our experiences will either authenticate or challenge our beliefs. The use of our experiences in this manner is closely tied with the fourth element of discerning truth—reason. We have the ability to use clear thinking and common sense in sorting out what to believe and what to leave behind. We use reason to meld together our experiences with a presumptive truth. If during this comparing and contrasting something does not reasonably fit, then our confidence in that belief will be shaken, leading us to keep exploring until we gain more clarity.

The fifth element, revelation, can be divided into two forms. The scriptures reveal God, nature reveals God, and God is certainly revealed to Christians by Jesus. Together, these components are often referred to as *general* revelation. Through these sources of revelation God moves people to know truth. But the greatest confidence and clarity that can be attained in a belief is demonstrated by what John Wesley referred to as his heart being strangely warmed. This is an example of *special* revelation, when God's self is disclosed more specifically to an individual for a special purpose. Special revelation is not something that can be called up or controlled. It is given to persons by an act of God's grace. However, by opening one's heart with an attitude that longs to hear God, the person acquiesces to the possibility.

The five sources of discovering truth—scripture, tradition, experience, reason, and revelation—are a valid way to approach understanding the Christian faith. When a truth emerges that does not contradict scripture, can be understood within the traditions formed by those before us, is congruent with our own and others' observed experiences, does not contradict reason, and is possibly received through special revelation, then we can deepen our commitment to that truth. However, knowing what we believe to be true of the faith is only the beginning. How our beliefs are embodied in our lives and direct our journeys is the real evidence of the beliefs we hold. If there is no evidence in our lives of a belief which we profess, then maybe we do not hold that belief strongly.

Beliefs often have a fragile beginning. A deep and trusting faith of any kind rarely comes quickly or untested. Instead, forming a belief is a process that usually begins with some amount of doubt or healthy skepticism. Consider this story:

> An aerialist, who specialized in riding a bicycle on a tightrope across waterfalls, set up his equipment across Niagara Falls. A great crowd gathered to watch him ride across the roaring waters. Not only did he complete the trip over, but he returned riding backwards! The crowd was in awe of his ability.
>
> He asked the crowd, "Do you believe I could do it again with a person sitting on my shoulders?" "Yes," they all shouted as one. "Which one of you will ride with me then?" he asked. No one spoke up.[8]

While the crowd's "Yes" was probably genuine, the real question is whether or not their belief was solid enough to influence their behavior. Beliefs can be genuine without being firmly held. Bringing our lives into harmony requires us to devote time to clarifying where we stand. When we feel free to encounter all our uplifting and painful experiences, our doubts and confidences, our detractors and supporters, in order to find truth, then the resulting integration will be a mature belief system. For Christians, a rational mind combined with a mind open to God's revelations blends into a powerful theological mosaic. This mosaic forms a wholeness that brings coherence to one's beliefs and enables one to navigate the many paradoxes faced in this life.

---

8. Burns, "Belief about or Belief in?" 6. Used by permission from Communication Resources, Inc.

2

Bible: What Are Its Origins and Use?

THE UNPARALLELED COURSE OF events set in motion at the birth of Jesus
Christ gave rise to the religion of Christianity. These events and their significance were recorded by the early followers of Jesus, their writings becoming the source of a unique body of literature now identified as the New
Testament of the Bible. However, events leading to the Christian faith began
long before the birth of Jesus and were recorded by people of the Jewish faith
from which the Christians emerged. This body of literature is now known to
Christians as the Old or First Testament and known to people of the Jewish
faith as the Hebrew Scriptures. This chapter will discuss how the sources of
these two texts, which now form the Christian Bible, came to be collected
and how they came to be the church's authoritative words for defining the
Christian faith. Since the words of these texts delineate the doctrines and
practices of Christianity, it is both important and enriching to understand
the path they took to reach us today.

The process was inordinately complex, and one chapter is insufficient
to cover all aspects. However, I will elucidate major historical steps, examine
some contemporary issues, and leave the rest to your further study with
some excellent resources found in the appendix. I endeavor to present veri-
fiable facts about this process and include evidence supporting these facts.
But there will also be times when we must admit that we lack hard evidence,
the answers to some of our questions having simply been lost to time, leaving gaps that await new evidence. However, what we currently know proves
very useful as it reveals historical and literary understandings that deepen
our ability to bring the intention of the texts to light.

Beginnings of Christians' Encounter with the Bible

Before we follow the trail of details about the origins of the Bible, we may want to consider what one expects to receive when one reads the Bible. The writers of the New Testament repeatedly speak of delivering what they received, with the hope we would receive it as well. Here are a few examples.

> For I received from the Lord what I also handed on to you. (1 Cor 11:23a)

> For I handed on to you as of first importance what I in turn had received. (1 Cor 15:3a)

And what was it that Jesus' disciples were receiving and handing on? We can glimpse a partial answer in the following record of Jesus' prayer to God.

> Now they [Jesus' disciples] know that everything you [God] have given me [Jesus] is from you; for the words that you gave to me I have given to them, and they have received them. (John 17:7–8a)

The Christian faith was transmitted through this receiving and handing on of the apostles' encounters with Jesus, including his words, works, death, and resurrection. Over time, the transmission of the message became increasingly tenuous as the apostles and their companions grew fewer, until none were left who could say they had seen and heard Jesus firsthand. However, their message was not lost, but was sustained as the convictions of the Christian faith spread both orally and via the writings left behind. These writings, compiled to form the New Testament of the Bible, pass on the tradition that was being delivered and remain the primary source for what Christians believe and endeavor to practice.

The word often used to refer to this message that was being *received and delivered* translates from the biblical Greek into English as *tradition*. In today's language, tradition is commonly thought of in terms of sentimental customs. However, such a definition is not a proper one for this use. Sentimental traditions are often an accumulation of customs that have been accepted because things have always been done in this way. With these time-honored traditions, conservatism is the goal, resistance to change is the norm, and proposed changes to them are often rejected with emotional responses. Some practices within today's churches embody this type of stagnating tradition, with the institutionalization of the church unwittingly giving rise to this vexing problem (more on this conundrum in chapters 6 and 7).

However, in stark contrast to holding on to the status quo of sentimental traditions, the tradition that Jesus was delivering to his disciples included new ideas that would not only change the practice of the established Jewish religion of their time, but also require a change in the life of his followers. Jesus did not discard the tradition contained in the Jewish people's sacred writings; he embraced the Jewish faith. His message expounded on these writings and illuminated that he was fulfilling the prophesy promised in them.

For those of the Jewish faith, the Hebrew Scriptures are the sacred writings of their community, recounting the history of ancient Israel, their trials and tribulations, and their way of life embodied in a set of moral and religious obligations and laws. For Christians, these sacred Hebrew writings bear witness to the promise of a savior, a promise fulfilled by Jesus. Throughout the New Testament Gospels, we read that Jesus cited the sacred writings of the Jewish people to illuminate and validate his mission.

For example, in the New Testament, Luke's Gospel recorded that Jesus read from a scroll of the Jewish sacred writings. The text he quoted is found beginning in chapter 61 of what we currently identify as the book of Isaiah in the Hebrew Scriptures or Old Testament. In this passage from Luke's Gospel, Jesus declares himself to be the anointed one, the one to fulfill those sacred words.

> When he [Jesus] came to Nazareth, where he had been brought up, he went to the synagogue on the sabbath day, as was his custom. He stood up to read, and the scroll of the prophet Isaiah was given to him. He unrolled the scroll and found the place where it was written:
> "The Spirit of the Lord is upon me, because he has anointed me to bring good news to the poor. He has sent me to proclaim release to the captives and recovery of sight to the blind, to let the oppressed go free, to proclaim the year of the Lord's favor."
> And he rolled up the scroll, gave it back to the attendant, and sat down. The eyes of all in the synagogue were fixed on him. Then he began to say to them, "Today this scripture has been fulfilled in your hearing." (Luke 4:16–21)

Again, in Luke's Gospel, we see a text that witnesses to Jesus as the expected and promised messiah of the Hebrew Scriptures. The reference in this text to *Moses and all the prophets* is commonly understood to be a reference to the early books of the Hebrew Scriptures.

> Then beginning with Moses and all the prophets, he [Jesus] in-
> terpreted to them the things about himself in all the scriptures.
> (Luke 24:27)

For Christians the New Testament does not supersede the Old Testament but is simply a continuation of the sacred writings. Together, the two
testaments define the Christian faith, inform God's people of the covenants
between God and humanity, and depict the realm that God desires to see
on earth. It is all one unfolding history as the Old Testament bears witness
to the promise of a savior, and the New Testament bears witness to Jesus as
this savior. These two parts of the Bible are also referred to by Christians as
the First Covenant and the Second Covenant, or the First Testament and the
New Testament, terms that more fully indicate a continuous history.

Although I digressed in order to elucidate how Christianity engages
the Bible, the core of this chapter is not about the message contained in the
scriptures or doctrines of the Christian and Jewish faiths, but is rather about
how the texts of the Bible were written, collected, and conferred authority.
The process through which the collection of books came to be recognized
as sacred scripture is called canonization. The final product of canonization,
namely the canon, refers to the books of the completed Bible.

There were many historic events that prompted the writing of the
manuscripts which became the Bible. There were also many circumstances
that prompted the religious leaders to feel compelled to confer official recognition on these manuscripts as sacred scripture. Jumping right to the conclusion of the canonization process, we can say that the stamp of approval
was not put on the canon of the Hebrew Scriptures (Old Testament) until
the end of the first century AD, and on the New Testament in AD 397. However, in the minds and practice of the leaders of the temple and the church,
the canon—the collection of books determined to contain God's inspired
words—was complete long before those dates.

Canonization

Before we trace the journey of these manuscripts, which were so carefully
written, transmitted, and translated, I will summarize which books were
chosen among the many to be included in the Bible. After this brief summary, I will describe the journeys that these books took. The twists and
turns of the canonization process hold intrigue for any historian and insight
and understanding for Christians.

Protestant Christians have followed the Jewish tradition, accepting
the twenty-four books of the Hebrew Scriptures as their Old Testament.

However, the content is arranged differently, and it is divided into thirty-nine books.[1] Roman Catholic and Orthodox Christians accepted not only these thirty-nine books, but interspersed the following among them—Tobit, Judith, Wisdom of Solomon, Ecclesiasticus, Baruch, the letter of Jeremiah, 1 Maccabees, 2 Maccabees, as well as additions to Esther and Daniel. These added books are referred to as deuterocanonical by those who accepted them into their Old Testament, thus distinguishing them from the thirty-nine protocanonical books. Protestant Bibles which include these additions out of ecumenical consciousness append them to the end of the Old Testament and refer to them as the Apocrypha. Those who recognize these books as apocryphal, or having doubtful authority, still consider them to be informative and valuable for study, but not appropriate for determining Christian doctrines

Even more books are included in Orthodox Bibles, and these are considered apocryphal by both Protestants and Catholics. These include 1 Esdras, Prayer of Manasseh, Psalm 151, 3 Maccabees, 2 Esdras, and 4 Maccabees. The majority of apocryphal literature was written between 200 BC and AD 50 and thus provides valuable knowledge of the period between the end of the Old Testament narrative and the beginning of the New Testament.

The New Testament process led to a less confounded outcome, although the process was no less complex. All Protestant, Catholic, and Orthodox Christians, have accepted the same twenty-seven books for the New Testament of their Bibles.[2]

The timeline graphs at the end of this chapter may be useful as you continue reading. They place, in relative order, the events described in the remainder of the chapter.

Let us now go back to the beginning. Writing systems developed as early as the fourth millennium BC in the lands where the history of the Bible unfolds. Written records became necessary as societies became more complex and needed records of diplomatic agreements as well as a means to transmit messages. The early writing systems were cumbersome and were the domain of trained scribes. There were some three hundred signs necessary to write Babylonian and some seven hundred symbols in the Egyptian

1. These thirty-nine books are: Genesis, Exodus, Leviticus, Numbers, Deuteronomy, Joshua, Judges, Ruth, 1 Samuel, 2 Samuel, 1 Kings, 2 Kings, 1 Chronicles, 2 Chronicles, Ezra, Nehemiah, Esther, Job, Psalms, Proverbs, Ecclesiastes, Song of Solomon, Isaiah, Jeremiah, Lamentations, Ezekiel, Daniel, Hosea, Joel, Amos, Obadiah, Jonah, Micah, Nahum, Habakkuk, Zephaniah, Haggai, Zechariah, Malachi.

2. These twenty-seven books are: Matthew, Mark, Luke, John, Acts of the Apostles, Romans, 1 Corinthians, 2 Corinthians, Galatians, Ephesians, Philippians, Colossians, 1 Thessalonians, 2 Thessalonians, 1 Timothy, 2 Timothy, Titus, Philemon, Hebrews, James, 1 Peter, 2 Peter, 1 John, 2 John, 3 John, Jude, Revelation.

hieroglyphic scripts. Scribes began to develop simpler systems which led to the Canaanite Linear script early in the second millennium BC. This script was composed of just over twenty letters rather than the hundreds of previous systems, and it was closely adaptable to the spoken word of the Canaanites. The Canaanite Linear script led to the development of the Phoenician letters used in the first millennium BC. The Phoenician alphabet was itself a precursor to the development and writing of the biblical languages of Hebrew, Aramaic, and Greek.

Early writing was carved by various means into the elements of stone and clay as reported in the following scripture verses.

> Then the Lord said to me, Take a large tablet and write on it in common characters. (Isa 8:1a)

> Then the Lord answered me and said: Write the vision; make it plain on tablets, so that a runner may read it. (Hab 2:2)

However, tablets were hard to carry and move around. Just as writing systems transitioned, so did writing materials. Soon media such as wood, wax on wood, leather, papyrus, parchment, and velum began to be preferred. Unfortunately, all writings have been subjected over time to deterioration and decay as well as the whims of humanity. It is important to understand that as a result, *we have no original documents of any biblical texts in our hands today.*

But that does not mean that the words did not survive. The reason for writing the sacred words down is the same reason we write anything down today. We write so words can be disseminated and preserved.

> Go now, write it before them on a tablet, and inscribe it in a book, so that it may be for the time to come as a witness forever. (Isa 30:8)

Although we tend to concentrate on the written word, we can also have confidence that the general public knew the texts by oral transmission as well, since there were a limited number of copies of the sacred texts. Scribes were an elite class who initially were the only ones who had access to the sacred scrolls. They made copies by hand, a lengthy and expensive process. During times of persecution many copies were destroyed, reducing the already limited number of written copies. But the texts themselves tell us that the importance was placed on preserving the information rather than the means of preservation.

So then, brothers and sisters, stand firm and hold fast to the traditions that you were taught by us, either by word of mouth or by our letter. (2 Thess 2:15)

Old Testament Canonization

The oldest known surviving evidence of words of the Old Testament are two very small silver scrolls dated to the sixth century BC. They contain the words of a priestly blessing found in the sixth chapter of Numbers which reads:

The Lord bless you and keep you; the Lord make his face to shine upon you, and be gracious to you; the Lord lift up his countenance upon you, and give you peace. (Num 6:24–26)

However, the earliest comprehensive Old Testament texts written in Hebrew that still exist today are the Codex Leningrad dated around AD 1008 and the even earlier leather and papyrus Dead Sea Scrolls. Discovered in 1946, the Dead Sea Scrolls contain representation from every book of the Hebrew Scriptures, except Esther, and precede the Codex Leningrad by at least eight centuries.

The Codex Leningrad was the product of a group of scholars and copyists known as the Masoretes. These scholars probably began their work of preserving the Hebrew scriptures as early as the seventh century AD and their work, known as the Masoretic Text, is the standard for the current Hebrew Scriptures and Old Testament texts.

The discovery of the Dead Sea Scrolls led to great anticipation about how closely the Masoretic Text compared to these much earlier copies of the texts. It was astounding that these newly discovered texts from the first or second century BC compared so closely to a work in the ninth century AD. This group of Jewish scholars had been meticulous in passing the tradition to later generations, a testimony to the high regard attached to these words.

It is not possible to attach a date to when the texts of the Old Testament were originally written or by whom. Methods using evidence from the text itself along with external evidence of documented historical events produce some clues but no absolute proof. The Old Testament covers a long period of time and probably includes some dependence on prior oral transmission. The primeval history of creation in Genesis eclipses direct human experience and precludes any confidence in dating the events from the narrative. The account of creation is followed by a historical context around 1500–1200 BC. Biblical history continues with the Israelites' trek from Egypt to

Canaan, which has been dated early in the Late Bronze Age. Israel's history continues to be expounded during the reigns of David and Solomon in the tenth century BC and through the time of the prophets of the sixth century BC. These dates are educated estimates resulting from the tedious work of biblical scholars using various methods of discovery. However, all we can say for certain is that the Old Testament is a literary collage produced by many authors and editors over a very long period of time. Even that information alone informs our reading of the scriptures.

Tracing the path of these books alongside history, we can begin when the northern kingdom of Israel was conquered by the Assyrians in the eighth century BC, scattering the Israelites. Another upheaval took place in 587 BC when the temple was destroyed by the Babylonians, and the Israelites were dispersed throughout the land of Babylon. Those who defeated them tried to destroy all copies of their sacred writings. Although we do not have a list of what documents the Assyrians and Babylonians were trying to destroy, the Israelites knew what to save. The manuscripts which were so important that they protected them with their lives were essentially the Israelites' canon of Hebrew Scripture at that point in time.

Further attesting to an early set of books considered sacred to the Jewish people are conversations recorded in the New Testament. Jesus and the apostles frequently made reference to scriptures. The Greek word translated as *scripture* in these New Testament texts specifically carries the meaning of writings of a divine and sacred sort.

> Then he [Jesus] opened their minds to understand the scriptures. (Luke 24:45)

> All scripture is inspired by God and is useful for teaching, for reproof, for correction, and for training in righteousness. (2 Tim 3:16)

In this next example the English word *scripture* is translated from the Greek phrase which literally says *this that stands written*, instead of the single Greek word for sacred writings.

> For I [Jesus] tell you, this scripture must be fulfilled in me. (Luke 22:37a)

Even this casual reference to scripture, *this that stands written*, must have brought to the readers' mind a particular set of writings. What it was that *stood written* would have been common knowledge to this society. Unfortunately, if a precise list of the books of the Hebrew Scriptures existed at the time of Jesus ministry, it is now lost to us. Other terms found in the

New Testament that point to the sacred Hebrew writings were *Moses and the prophets, the Law and prophets, the Law, the writings,* and *the psalms.*

> Then he said to them, "These are my words that I spoke to you while I was still with you—that everything written about me in the law of Moses, the prophets, and the psalms must be fulfilled." Then he [Jesus] opened their minds to understand the scriptures. (Luke 24:44–45)
>
> "Do not think that I [Jesus] have come to abolish the law or the prophets; I have come not to abolish but to fulfill." (Matt 5:17)

With so many important references made by Jesus and the apostles to scripture, particularly passages which foretold of a savior coming to earth, Christians certainly have an interest in identifying the content of these Hebrew Scriptures.

It is commonly considered, but without absolute evidence, that the Hebrew Scriptures were collected and determined to be sacred in three stages. However, it is impossible to say who chose the books in each stage and who assigned authority to them. The first stage, the Law, or writings of Moses, includes the first five books of the Old Testament—Genesis, Exodus, Leviticus, Numbers, and Deuteronomy. This first of three sections is referred to as the Torah and the final edit and closing of this section was probably completed after Cyrus allowed the Israelites to return from their Babylonian exile in 538 BC. The next section was the Prophets, whose history ends late in the third century BC. The last section, the Writings, which includes the remaining books of the Hebrew Scriptures, would have been determined by or before the first century AD.

There was a final push to close the canon of the Hebrew Scriptures as the Jewish community was rebuilding after its collapse and scattering following the destruction of the temple by the Romans in AD 70. Perhaps the momentum for canonization came from a fear of losing the history or teachings that had guided their lives for so long. Or maybe the driving force was concern over the use of the Hebrew Scriptures in preaching that Jesus, the long-awaited Messiah, had arrived. Whatever the reason, during the first and early part of the second century, a gathering of rabbinic scholars in Jamnia carried on discussions concerning many topics germane to Jewish life, one of which was delineating the books which made up the Hebrew Scriptures. The books of the Law and Prophets appeared to already be established when these discussions were taking place. However, the final set of books, the Writings, was still being discussed. As no change was declared from these discussions, it appears an already known compilation of twenty-four books remained as the canon of the Hebrew Bible.

As already mentioned, when Jesus exchanged views with Jewish theologians in the synagogues he often appealed to the scriptures. It is apparent both parties equally acknowledged which books constituted scripture and accepted the sacred authority of these words. When we find scriptures quoted by Jesus or the disciples, we can work backwards to identify the reference from the Hebrew Scriptures. Following is an example of a pairing from the New and Old Testament. First Jesus quotes scripture:

> So the Pharisees and the scribes asked him [Jesus], "Why do your disciples not live according to the tradition of the elders, but eat with defiled hands?" He said to them, "Isaiah prophesied rightly about you hypocrites, as it is written,
> 'This people honors me with their lips, but their hearts are far from me; in vain do they worship me, teaching human precepts as doctrines.'
> "You abandon the commandment of God and hold to human tradition." (Mark 7:5–8)

We can find that referenced passage in the Old Testament book of Isaiah:

> The Lord said: Because these people draw near with their mouths and honor me with their lips, while their hearts are far from me, and their worship of me is a human commandment learned by rote. (Isa 29:13)

When lists of the names of the books that are included in the Hebrew Scriptures began to appear among leaders of the Christian church, there were some discrepancies. The first list that survives today was written by Melito, bishop of Sardis. This list was preserved in the writings of Eusebius (c. 260–340), bishop of Caesarea. It is thought that Melito obtained his list from a Jewish source in Palestine around AD 170. According to Eusebius, Melito wrote, "Having learned accurately the books of the old covenant, I set them down and have sent them to you. These are their names."[3] Although there must be some interpretation of his list of books since some have been grouped together, it appears he has included all the books of the current Hebrew Scriptures except Esther.

Another list, also preserved by Eusebius, was compiled by Origen (c. 185–254), who is often considered the greatest biblical scholar of his time. Origen is quoted as writing: "We should not be ignorant that there are twenty-two books of the [Old] Testament, according to the tradition of the

---

3. Bruce, *Canon of Scripture*, 71.

Hebrews."[4] He followed this introduction with a list of these books, which was very close to the final twenty-four of the Hebrew Scriptures.

Likewise, Athanasius (c. 296–373), bishop of Alexandria, who was the first to use the term *canon*, wrote: "It has seemed good to me . . . to set forth in order the books which are included in the canon and have been delivered to us with accreditation that they are divine."[5] This statement is again followed by a list of Old Testament books. Origen and Athanasius' lists are very similar. They contain the same number of books, although Origen combines Ruth and Judges into one book and Athanasius omits Esther. What we can take away from the examples of these lists is that identifying a canon of Hebrew Scriptures was certainly one of the goals of the early Christian scholars and there was some fluidity in what books were considered authoritative and how they were collected and ordered.

One illustration of this fluidity, which ultimately contributed to the differences in the Roman Catholic and Protestant Old Testament canon, is the history of the Septuagint.[6] The Septuagint was a third and second century BC translation of the Hebrew Scriptures into Greek by Jewish scholars in Alexandria. This translation was the consequence of the spread of the Greek culture around the Mediterranean Sea and eastward following Alexander the Great's conquests, and the dispersion of the Jewish people into these areas. For those around Alexandria, Greek was becoming their first language and without this translation they would have lost access to the Hebrew Scriptures. The use of the Septuagint quickly spread throughout the Greek speaking world and was most likely the version of scripture used by many of the Jewish people who became followers of Jesus.

One example of the Septuagint's use can be gleaned from an account of Stephen in the New Testament book of Acts. Acts 7:14 reports that when Stephen, a follower of Jesus, was questioned by the high priest, he spoke in his defense by repeating narratives from the Old Testament. In his narrative, Stephen states the number of Jacob's relatives is seventy-five.

> Then Joseph sent and invited his father Jacob and all his relatives to come to him, seventy-five in all. (Acts 7:14)

Seventy-five is the number reported in the Greek Septuagint versions of Genesis and Exodus.[7] However, the Hebrew texts of Genesis and Exodus count Jacob's people as seventy, as shown below.

4. Bruce, *Canon of Scripture*, 73.

5. Bruce, *Canon of Scripture*, 78.

6. The Septuagint is often represented by the Roman numerals LXX.

7. Durham, *Word Biblical Commentary*, 2.

> The children of Joseph, who were born to him in Egypt, were two; all the persons of the house of Jacob who came into Egypt were seventy. (Gen 46:27)

> The total number of people born to Jacob was seventy. Joseph was already in Egypt. (Exod 1:5)

This clearly shows there was use of the Septuagint during the lifetime of the apostles. Further, some words attributed to Paul, a Greek speaking Jew from Tarsus, are likewise closer to the Septuagint than the Hebrew.

There is another significant aspect of the Septuagint that needs to be discussed. It concerns the extent of the collection of books it contained. Originally, it was composed of only the first five books of the Hebrew Scriptures. Gradually all the books of the Hebrew Scriptures were included. But it did not stop there. Additional books were translated into Greek and added to the collection of the Septuagint. These are the books that became the deuterocanonical and apocryphal books of the Roman Catholic and Orthodox churches. Most of these apocryphal books are Greek translations of Hebrew manuscripts that the Jewish scholars did not consider to be sacred.

There was yet another aspect of the Septuagint that left its mark on history. The followers of Jesus, who happened to be Greek speaking Jews, preached from the Septuagint to zealously spread the message of Jesus being the fulfillment of Israel's long-awaited Messiah. As with any translation, word choices can be critical, and some felt the Septuagint chose words that more closely fit their belief that Jesus was the Messiah. As a result, the Jews who did not believe Jesus to be the Messiah began to shy away from the Septuagint and prefer the Hebrew Scriptures.

As we move along to the year AD 200, we see Latin replacing Greek throughout the Roman Empire. As could be expected, there was soon a Latin translation of the Septuagint. It was, however, an unsatisfactory translation and Jerome (c. 347–420), a biblical scholar, was asked to revise this Latin translation. Jerome began his task with the Septuagint as his primary source, but soon realized that this was not sufficient. So, he began again. This time he primarily used the Hebrew texts with the help of Jewish teachers. Although Jerome took issue with the additional books of the Septuagint, those outside of the Hebrew Scriptures, he included them in his Latin translation. However, he continued to argue that these extra books, while informative and valuable for study, were not appropriate for determining Christian doctrines.

Jerome's contemporary, Augustine (354–430), did not share Jerome's lack of confidence in the apocryphal books as sacred documents. In AD 397 the Third Council of Carthage came to a consensus that matched Augustine's

list and the apocryphal books became a part of the Old Testament. ɪ
mid 1500s the Council of Trent stated their approval of Jerome's AD ̚,
Latin translation, now known as the Vulgate, which included the deuteroca
nonical (apocryphal) books, as authorized for the Roman Catholic Church.

Moving ahead to the Protestant Reformation, we find that once again
the canon of scripture becomes a topic of concern. Theologian Martin
Luther (1483–1546), sometimes referred to as the *father of the Protestant
Reformation*, questioned many of the church's practices, particularly indulgences. Indulgences were a practice in the Roman Catholic Church which
collected financial contributions, claiming that these contributions would
aid that person after death to move from purgatory to heaven. When Luther
sought the scriptural sources for this practice, they were found in the apocryphal books—the very books Jerome concluded were not to be used for
establishing the authority of ecclesiastical (church) dogmas. Pair this with
Luther's insistence on *sola scriptura*, that scripture alone, not scripture plus
church tradition (which included indulgences), is the source of Christian
revelation, and once again the validity of the apocryphal books as scripture
was questioned. Thus, Jerome's caution about these books was given cre-
dence, as Protestants removed the apocryphal books from their Bibles.

There were many theologians, councils, and scholars who contributed
to the canonization of the Christians' Old Testament, and I hope this brief
narrative has sufficiently produced a sense and understanding of the process. To summarize, at the beginning of the Christian church, there was
already a recognizable canon of scripture, namely the Hebrew Scriptures
of the Jewish people. These were the books so carefully preserved by the
Masoretes, which ultimately became the thirty-nine books in common to all
Christians' Old Testaments. What made these words sacred was the belief
that they were inspired by God.

New Testament Canonization

The New Testament canonization covers a much shorter period of time than
the formation of the Old Testament, but the trail left for us to follow is just as
overgrown and winding. The oldest fragment of the New Testament still in
existence today is a small (2.5 inch by 3.5 inch) piece of papyrus, containing
a few verses of John's Gospel, that was discovered in Egypt. It has been dated
to around AD 125. As far as can be worked out, the original writings of the
New Testament were written over a relatively short period of forty to fifty
years, beginning as early as the early 50s AD.

' fragments of papyri that help scholars piece together
and there are also more-complete fourth-century
ce on parchment (a refined use of animal skins). Two
'e in codex or book format (as opposed to scrolls)
Codex Sinaiticus and Codex Vaticanus. They are
_ copies of the Old and New Testament written in Greek. The
_..ny of the codex Sinaiticus is currently in the British Library and the
codex Vaticanus resides in the Vatican library.

The new discovery of an ancient manuscript can pose a challenge to our current Bibles and make it seem that the process still has a few loose ends. Some feel that this uncertainty mars the sacredness of the Bible and wish that we would do away with all the academic considerations. However, this aspiration for integrity and accuracy provides reassurance that our Bible consists of texts that are paramount in accurately delivering its message.

The path of collecting and authorizing the New Testament books from manuscripts produced by those who were eyewitnesses to this new movement of God began in the late first and early second century. Theologians whom we now recognize as apostolic or church fathers took up this task. The earliest apostolic fathers came from different geographic areas and from different cultures, both Jewish and Hellenistic. As they were heavily influenced by the apostles in both their writings and their thoughts, it is believed that there was at least some personal contact between the early apostolic fathers and the apostles. While reviewing the apostolic fathers' writings, we can observe the incubation of the New Testament canon. As they began to write, Christian theology and the church were advanced. Further, the sources they used to form their theology began to take on an authoritative air.

These sources included Paul's letters, which were gathered into a collection and circulated among the churches. At the same time, a sorting of which gospels carried authority began to emerge. As these and other authoritative sources began to be collected, the formation of the New Testament was underway. We can review the contributions of a few of these apostolic fathers to give a sense of this development.

Often called the first apostolic father, Clement of Rome was the pope of Rome from the year 88 until he died in AD 99. It is believed he had contact with the disciple Peter; it has even been proposed that Clement was conferred a pope by Peter. Clement's Bible was the Old Testament. His writings often quoted from those books, and he prefaced his quotes by identifying them as scripture. He also quoted the words of Jesus with phrases that we currently find in the Gospels, and he also shows knowledge of some of Paul's epistles. But unlike his Old Testament references, he does not refer to any of these as scripture. However, he regards them highly and uses them in his arguments as having some authority, particularly the words of Jesus. This is the beginning of identifying which writings would ultimately be deemed authoritative and canonized into the New Testament.

Ignatius (c. 35–107) was a bishop of Antioch who wrote a number of letters that revealed Christian theology. Like Clement, he was familiar with many of Paul's epistles and some of the Gospels, and his Old Testament references are prefaced to indicate they are scripture. Even though he does not refer to the Gospels or Paul's letters as scripture, he does single out and give special place to the early writings that tell of the resurrection of Jesus. Jesus Christ was his seat of authority.

Papias (c. 60–130) was bishop of Hierapolis in Phrygia. His preference for learning about Jesus' ministry was from "a living and surviving voice,"[8] or oral rather than written sources. There is no evidence that he was familiar with Paul's epistles. However, he does seem to lean somewhat on John's Gospel. He was probably developing his theology from the words of Palestinian Christians who moved to Asia Minor after the AD 70 fall of Jerusalem. This is the beginning of the end of passing on the traditions orally. Dependence on written accounts will now become the common mode of transmission among theologians. He also leaves us evidence that Mark's Gospel was a recording of Peter's telling.

Polycarp (c. 69–155) was the bishop of Smyrna. He defended Christianity with writings from the time when the disciples and apostles were still living. He, like others of his day, did not formally assign authority to these early writings, but ascribed a special status to them and gave them priority over the writings of the apostolic fathers which came later. At this point there is beginning to be a more distinct demarcation of which writings were to be trusted as representing authentic Christianity. It is also a time when heretical writings and misinterpretations are beginning to appear.

Polycarp defended against a heretical sect who were followers of Marcion. Marcion (d. c. 160) provided his followers with a set of "holy scriptures" which did not include the Old Testament, for Marcion rejected the God of the Old Testament, claiming it was not the same God as the one Jesus revealed. He also held to a belief that Jesus was not born, but supernaturally descended. Marcion included in his holy scriptures a Gospel of Luke and a collection of ten of Paul's epistles including Galatians, a combined 1 and 2 Corinthians, Romans, combined 1 and 2 Thessalonians, Ephesians (which he named Laodiceans), Colossians, Philippians, and Philemon. However, and this is a big however, these copies were heavily edited by Marcion. Any text that did not align with his beliefs was edited out. For example, his

---

8. Metzger, *Canon of the New Testament*, 52.

version of the Gospel of Luke did not include the birth story of Jesus, or the genealogy of Jesus back to Adam, or any quote of Jesus fulfilling Old Testament prophecy, or any text that included quotes from Old Testament books. He used the same type of editing to expunge Paul's epistles of anything that contradicted his beliefs.

The unintended consequence of Marcion's heretical "bible" was to accelerate the canonization of the New Testament. The apostolic fathers were now not only busy identifying legitimate Christian writings and expounding the faith, but they were also trying to limit perversions of the faith. Marcion's bible was not called a New Testament, but he had unleashed the idea of collecting and assigning authority to the writings that impart the Christian faith.

The church has often been accused of selecting the manuscripts which promoted a theology of their choosing. In many ways, this assertion is true, but the church need not apologize for this focus. The texts they were selecting were those that represented the faith to which Jesus and the apostles attested. The limits of selection were placed around the central unifying message of faith in Jesus as man, Jesus as Christ, sent from God, and exalted in death. These limits result in the distinctiveness which defines Christianity. Although they selected books which represented the unifying message of Christ, these same manuscripts also represented diverse expressions of the faith. This diversity will be discussed more fully in following chapters.

The apostolic fathers were aware that there were beginning to be subsequent manuscripts that were not true to the unifying message of Christ, and they attempted to make known which ones these were. Irenaeus (c. 130–200) recognized the perversion of the faith by the emerging heretical movement of Gnosticism. In his work *Against Heresies*, Irenaeus expounded on the Gnostics' beliefs which did not align with the apostles' teachings. Gnosticism did not have centralized leadership, and beliefs varied among groups of Gnostics, making it difficult to delineate their heretical teachings. In 1947 a library of Gnostic literature was discovered which more completely detailed the heresies that Irenaeus pointed out.

This collection of Gnostic literature, discovered in Upper Egypt, is referred to as the Nag Hammadi Library. Although these unearthed documents are from the fourth century, they appear to have been copied from second and early-third-century originals. One of the most consistent heresies of this group was the belief that they held privately revealed knowledge which was available only to them. To Christianity, one of the most discordant Gnostic beliefs was the belief in a subordinate God. This *demiurge*, in Gnostic thought, is the God of the Old Testament who created a corrupt material world and is not the same God who came to earth in Jesus Christ.

Because of their high reverence for Christ and the spiritual world, they felt entitled to call themselves Christians. However, many of their ideas were not congruent or compatible with the tradition of Jesus Christ and the apostles. Their writings often borrowed from the New Testament Gospels and books but with slight, yet very significant, alterations, making their distortions difficult to recognize by the uninitiated. These altered writings no doubt instilled in the apostolic fathers a need to produce a canon of scripture.

Tertullian (160–225) also wrote against several heresies, including those of Marcion and Gnosticism. Tertullian recognized and exhorted that one is in dangerous territory when one removes references that do not conform to one's opinion or when texts are discomposed in such a way as to lead to misinterpretation. These cautions to prevent wandering off into a heresy are just as valid today as in the time of the apostolic fathers.

By this time there was a good idea of which texts to consider for canonization. They were the ones being trusted in discussions by the apostolic fathers and being read during worship alongside the Old Testament Scriptures. Remember the earliest Christians were Jews and they had not given up the practices of their heritage. The Hebrew Scriptures continued to be read when they gathered, but now added to these readings were Paul's letters, the Gospels, and other writings that would later become our New Testament. The canon of the New Testament, emerging from first-century documents, was taking shape in this period of early-second-century practices. Those groups that read, copied, and passed around these writings developed into mature churches as the faith spread.

But there was, as yet, no canon. The apostolic fathers were striving to preserve the authentic tradition received from Christ and the apostles by identifying and preserving the documents that reflected the purest form of the faith. They understood that they needed to confront the arising philosophies that threatened to sever Christianity's rootedness in Jesus Christ. In response to these concerns, they developed a *rule of faith* which circulated in the second century. This precursor to doctrinal creeds set down the essential contents of the Christian faith and would be used to distinguish the orthodox tradition from heresies and guide the selection of authoritative manuscripts.

One important piece of evidence of the canonization process left to us is the Muratorian Document, discovered in 1740. It is a copy of a document that most probably originated at the end of the second century and contains a list of books recognized as authorized by the Roman church. These books were considered paramount in establishing the doctrine and practice of the faith and included twenty-one of the twenty-seven books in our New Testament. Even more valuable were the comments it included about each book, which lead us to understand that a primary consideration for including them as authorized is that their origins can be traced to eyewitnesses of Jesus and firsthand accounts of the apostles. Those who had been with Jesus were considered to advance the inspired words of God. The authors of the New Testament books did not write with the purpose of creating a collection of books that would become the New Testament, or even with the purpose of their writings becoming known as scripture. They were simply writing to expound, spread, and preserve the message of Jesus.

While firsthand knowledge of Jesus' words by the apostles would become the primary criteria for inclusion of a book in the canon, conforming to the rule of faith (orthodoxy) was also essential, as was a consensus of acceptance of the texts among the churches. As the canon of the New Testament progressed, it became a matter of paring down, not building up, a list of books to include. There were many documents written by the apostolic fathers that were circulated among the churches which contained sound theology that conformed to the rule of faith, but these were not included because they were far removed from the source of the apostles' words, which were considered inspired by God.

Various theologians each made their own list of authoritative books. A collection of Paul's letters circulated among the churches and gained early recognition. This acceptance was followed closely by a consensus of inclusion of the three Gospels, Matthew, Mark, and Luke. The Gospel of John joined this set of Gospels after it was disentangled from the Gnostics. As consensus grew, more refined lists were produced. However, it was Athanasius who first produced a list of the twenty-seven books that would become our New Testament, just as he had produced a near complete list of the accepted Old Testament books. The books recognized by those early churches still needed an official stamp of approval. It was Augustine's list, which mirrored that of Athanasius and mirrored the books being read in the churches, that was carried to the Third Council of Carthage in AD 397 and set the limits of the canon of the Bible with the following words:

> . . . it is resolved that nothing should be read in church under the name of the divine scriptures except the canonical writings. The canonical writings, then, are these: . . . of the New Testament: [followed by a listing of the twenty-seven books currently in our Bibles].[9]

This official declaration did not end all discussion. The inclusion of some books in the canon were again questioned during the Reformation and a

---

9. Bruce, *Canon of Scripture*, 233.

few churches still do not read from all twenty-seven books. However, the canon has withstood the test of time and argument and has officially remained unchanged.

Transmission of the Texts

As modern readers, we are privileged to have the convenience of holding in our hands a book which presents the scriptures to us in our own language in an orderly fashion that can be easily referenced. The Bible did not originate with a convenient numbering system. Chapters were a thirteenth-century development and verses were not added until the sixteenth. The earliest texts did not use punctuation, and the source documents for the New Testament did not even have spaces between the words.

We can thank the diligence of scribes, scholars, and linguists that the sacred texts have survived and passed to us in such a serviceable format. But the texts have not survived as perfect copies of the originals. The repeated copying by human scribes resulted in manuscripts that have introduced some uncertainties. Try copying, in longhand, a few pages of printed text and pass that to another person to copy and you can appreciate the problems inherent in accurately transmitting manuscripts.

These variants, introduced by human hands, initiate the need to discuss three terms associated with the scriptures: infallibility, inerrancy, and authority. Although scholarly textual critics recognize that errors and variants have been introduced during transmission, Christians still understand the Bible to be infallible. What exactly does that mean? Biblical infallibility, properly understood, simply means that the Bible will not fail in the purpose God has for it. It does not mean that we hold perfect copies of word-for-word, God-written texts. Saying this does not preclude the view of the Bible containing God's inspired words. Perhaps the variances in the scriptures, the scribal errors, and the array of interpretations of the Bible are God's way of keeping before us the need to carefully listen to the words of scripture in their entire context.

Closely associated with infallibility is the idea of inerrancy. It is sometimes claimed that inerrancy means that scripture is free from all error. However, inconsistencies can be identified throughout the Bible. Consider the number of soldiers reported in David's army as found in these accounts:

> Joab reported to the king the number of those who had been recorded: in Israel there were eight hundred thousand soldiers able to draw the sword, and those of Judah were five hundred thousand. (2 Sam 24:9)

> Joab gave the total count of the people to David. In all Israel there were one million one hundred thousand men who drew the sword, and in Judah four hundred seventy thousand who drew the sword. (1 Chr 21:5)

Also consider the inconsistences between the Gospel writers in the following three accounts concerning the number of women at Christ's tomb.

> When the sabbath was over, Mary Magdalene, and Mary the mother of James, and Salome bought spices, so that they might go and anoint him. And early on the first day of the week, when the sun had risen, they went to the tomb. (Mark 16:1–2)

> After the sabbath, as the first day of the week was dawning, Mary Magdalene and the other Mary went to see the tomb. (Matt 28:1)

> But on the first day of the week, at early dawn, they came to the tomb, taking the spices that they had prepared and returning from the tomb, they told all this to the eleven and to all the rest. Now it was Mary Magdalene, Joanna, Mary the mother of James, and the other women with them who told this to the apostles. (Luke 24:1, 9–10)

Denying that there are inconsistencies in the narratives throughout the Bible would be indefensible. Sometimes there is an attempt to promote the inerrancy of the Bible in all subjects, including such things as science and history. This claim is difficult to support given the knowledge that we currently have about our world and the universe, especially when we recognize that the authors of the scripture made extensive use of allegory, imagery, and metaphors when relating to God's nature. The concept of inerrancy is probably best relegated to those aspects of scripture which encompass and describe the relationship between God and humanity.

When God's words are read, Christians believe that the authority of God directs and strengthens God's people to bring about God's will. Bringing God's kingdom to earth is *the authority of scripture* in action. Unfortunately, whose authority it is can be lost in the heat of argument. It is God's authority, not humanity's, that Christians strive to hear in the words of the Bible. When a case is made based on "the Bible says," often cherry picking a single or small selection of verses, it should be a red flag that cautions us. If reading those verses in context does not confirm the argument, we may question whose authority is actually being invoked. It is tempting to try to usurp God's authority to promote one's own ideas. We must accept the perplexity that, although sacred and inspired by God, the text of scripture has been pressed into service by the hearts and minds of humans and can be subject to their motives.

So, there is evidence of scribal errors and variations as copies of copies were made. The variants that were introduced by scribes appear to be to correct grammar, clarify a passage, or even bring it into line with some other copy of the manuscript, or for other reasons we can only surmise. Because of the errors and variants, it is important to continue to study all available manuscripts in an attempt to construct a text as close to the original uncorrupted version as possible. Correcting scribal errors is not taken lightly. It requires an understanding of the entire Bible, extensive knowledge of the biblical languages, and a grasp of ancient Near Eastern culture so that the intended meaning is preserved.

Let us examine one of the better-known passages in the Bible to demonstrate how the process of establishing the text as near to the original as possible is practiced. Matthew 6:13 is the conclusion of what has become known as the Lord's Prayer. The King James Version of the Bible reads:

> And lead us not into temptation, but deliver us from evil: For thine is the kingdom, and the power, and the glory, for ever. Amen. (Matt 6:13, KJV)

However, as a result of consulting more reliable Greek manuscripts, such as the Codex Sinaiticus and Codex Vaticanus, where the final doxology, or words of praise ("For thine is the kingdom, and the power, and the glory, for ever"), were absent, the doxology was removed from later English translations. There is even a manuscript, Codex 1424, from the ninth or tenth century that includes a note which states, "The 'because yours is the kingdom' to 'amen' is not found in some copies."[10] Reflecting on the mounting evidence, a more recent English translation, the New Revised Standard Version, chose to remove the doxology from the text and disclose this variant in a footnote. Matthew 6:13 in the NRSV reads as follows:

> And do not bring us to the time of trial, but rescue us from the evil one. (Matt 6:13)

The corresponding footnote to this verse reads:

> Other ancient authorities add, in some form, *For the kingdom and the power and the glory are yours forever. Amen.*[11]

---

10. Hagner, *Word Biblical Commentary*, 144.

11. Metzger and Murphy, *New Oxford Annotated Bible*, NT 9.

The addition of the doxology to the prayer by a scribe was most likely a result of it having been included in liturgies of the church when the prayer was recited. Perhaps a scribe heard the final doxology over and over in the worshiping community and so added it to the text he was working on, and it was then carried forward with each subsequent copy. Or perhaps the doxology was jotted in the margins of a copy the scribe was copying, and he inserted it into the text. We will probably never know.

This variant is but one that the editors thought was important to document. However, the *Nestle-Aland Greek New Testament*, which strives to document as many existing manuscripts as possible, records thousands of variants that are not recorded in our English Bibles.[12] All the available fragments and variants are considered and weighed by scholars in order to establish the most reliable edition of the Bible for our use. It is remarkable that the major Christian doctrines do not depend on any variant text. We can trust that the diverse manuscripts which compose the Bible have consistently articulated the same message through the years of transmission.

Translations of the Biblical Texts

Efforts continue to not only maintain accuracy in biblical texts, but also to make the sacred texts readily accessible. Unrestricted accessibility is most effectively accomplished by translating the Bible into current vernacular languages and producing and distributing more copies. The widespread use of the printing press, beginning in the 1500s, certainly helped produce more copies. As mentioned earlier, translations quickly proved necessary with one of the first translations, the Septuagint, occurring when the Hebrew Scriptures were translated into Greek. This process of translation to the common language of the time and region has been repeated all over the world, and there are now Bibles available in over five hundred languages. Following are a few examples of translations that hold importance for many of us today.

Vulgate

The Vulgate, as already discussed is an AD 405 Latin translation by the biblical scholar Jerome. The Hebrew language texts were the source for the Vulgate's Old Testament, the Greek Septuagint for the apocryphal books, and Greek sources were used for the New Testament. In 1546 the Roman Catholic Church ratified the Vulgate as their Bible.

12. Aland et al., *Nestle-Aland Novum Testamentum Graece.*

King James Version (also known as the Authorized Version)

The translation known as the King James Version (KJV) was published in 1611. Capitalizing on the use of the printing press was an important step in providing this version of the biblical text to the increasing masses of English literates. However, as we saw earlier in this chapter, the basis for the KJV was not from documents as close to the source as possible, resulting in a less than ideal version of the Bible. The New Testament of the KJV was primarily translated from a 1535 reconstruction of Greek documents known as the *Texus Receptus*. This text relied heavily on late-tenth to twelfth-century copies of Greek documents, even though many earlier Greek documents, deemed more reliable than those used in the *Texus Receptus,* were available. For the Old Testament, the translators of the KJV primarily used the Hebrew Scriptures.

Over fifty scholars, including Hebrew and Greek professors from Oxford and Cambridge, contributed to the KJV. Considering the late material used as a source text, the KJV is remarkably accurate. However, future efforts to publish an English version closer to the original manuscripts were inevitable.

Despite the flaws in the KJV, it remains the Bible of choice for many Christians today. One reason for its continued popularity may be that the translating scholars were well-versed in Hebrew and to a large degree were able to retain the poetic style of the text. This task was not an easy one, considering that the two languages, English and Hebrew, are very different. Retaining the rhythm of the original Hebrew has provided some beautiful and enriching language to express one's faith. Take as an example the familiar Psalm 23.

The 1568 *Bishops' Bible* was an official English version of the Bible at the time the KJV committee began their translation. Note the language of verses 1–2 of Psalm 23:

> God is my sheepheards, therefore I can lacke nothing: he wyll cause me to repose my selfe in pasture full of grasse, and he wyll leade me vnto calme waters.[13]

Which would appear as below if we were to use current English spellings:

> God is my shepherd, therefore I can lack nothing: he will cause me to repose myself in pastures full of grass, and he will lead me unto calm waters.

Now read the flowing poetic language of the King James Version:

13. *Bishops' Bible,* 300.

> The Lord is my shepherd; I shall not want. He maketh me to lie
> down in green pastures: he leadeth me beside the still waters.
> (Ps 23:1–2, KJV)

This poetic style has been carried forward into the more recent New Revised
Standard Version, a testimony to the important contribution made by the
King James Version. It reads:

> The Lord is my shepherd, I shall not want. He makes me lie down
> in green pastures; he leads me beside still waters. (Ps 23:1–2)

New Revised Standard Version

The New Revised Standard Version (NRSV), published in 1989, is a familiar
and widely used English translation that took advantage of the Old and New
Testament and apocryphal source documents that are outlined below (or
the earlier editions available at the time of their work). It was authorized by
an ecumenical team that included representation from Protestant, Roman
Catholic, Eastern Orthodox, and Jewish scholars. It is a good translation for
biblical studies and is written at an eleventh grade reading level. An excellent summary from an article by Bruce M. Metzger traces the history that
led to the creation and publication of the NRSV:

> The New Revised Standard Version of the Bible is an authorized
> revision of the Revised Standard Version, published in 1952,
> which was a revision of the American Standard Version, pub-
> lished in 1901, which, in turn, embodied earlier revisions of the
> King James Version, published in 1611.[14]

There is also a New Revised Standard Version, Catholic Edition (NRSV-CE)
that includes the deuterocanonical books in the traditional Catholic order.

The New American Bible and Revised Edition

The New American Bible (NAB) is the English-language Catholic Bible approved for use at Mass in the United States. The Revised Edition (NABRE),
released in 2010, includes major updates of both the Old and New Testaments and is approved for private study by Catholics, but not for liturgical
use. It is written at a seventh grade reading level and made use of the source
documents described below.

14. Metzger, "To the Reader," ix.

The New International Version

The 1984 publication of the New International Version (NIV) quickly became popular for its easy-to-read seventh grade language level. It also used the reliable source documents listed below. This version was updated in 2005 and renamed Today's New International Version (TNIV). Since that time, both the 1984 NIV and the 2005 TNIV have been phased out and will no longer be published. Their 2011 replacement takes the same name as the 1984 edition, New International Version (NIV), but is a rewrite which retains some of the 1984 NIV translation and some of the 2005 TNIV translation. A study of the controversies associated with these versions is beyond the scope of this chapter, but if researched, it will shed light on a few of the reasons we have so many versions of the Bible on the market today and how critical word choices can be in a translation. It is the nature of translations that none are perfect, and thus, it is not surprising that no single translation satisfies all groups of readers.

Common English Bible

One of the newest English translations is the Common English Bible (CEB). Its 2011 publication includes the Old and New Testaments as well as the deuterocanonical books. It is an academically excellent translation from the reliable sources listed below, is written in a comfortable eighth grade level of English, uses gender-inclusive language where appropriate, and includes contractions, a feature that contributes to its natural sound when read aloud.

Present Day Sources

Old Testament Source Documents

The current standard for translation and analysis of the Old Testament is the Hebrew Masoretic Text, as found in *Biblia Hebraica Stuttgartensia*, along with a few texts from an earlier time, including the Dead Sea Scrolls. As described earlier in this chapter, the Massoretes were Jewish scholars and grammarians who preserved these sacred texts. As part of their work, they introduced vowel points and accents to aid in pronunciation at a time when the use of this form of Hebrew was diminishing, and they also included notes in the margins which preserved variants or added other useful explanations.

Deuterocanonical and Apocryphal Source Documents

The deuterocanonical and apocryphal books are part of the Old Testament for Roman Catholic and Orthodox Christians. As discussed earlier, Jewish and Protestant scriptures do not include these books. The 1935 publication of Alfred Rahlfs's edition of the Septuagint, the *Göttingen Septuagint*, and a second-century translation of portions of the Septuagint by Theodotion, are the primary sources for translations of these books.

New Testament Source Documents

All texts that are included in the New Testament were originally written in Greek. Today translators and others who want to analyze the biblical texts are fortunate to have a Greek source for the New Testament, namely the twenty-eighth edition of the *Nestle-Aland Novum Testamentum Graece* published in 2011. This critical text of the Greek New Testament is the work of many scholars who have compared the available manuscripts to determine the reading closest to the original. It also documents, through a critical apparatus and extensive footnotes, variants of the manuscripts. Contemporary analysis and translations of the New Testament are greatly enhanced by the availability of this modern-day standard of Greek source documents.

Translations Abound

Beginning in the 1900s there has been a proliferation of new translations of the Bible into English, with accuracy and clarity as the driving forces. The discovery of texts closer to the original source and ongoing biblical studies have prompted efforts to improve accuracy. Clarity is always a moving target since English is a living language. Over time unfamiliar vocabulary and archaic grammar must be overhauled. Not everyone agrees on how these two improvements are best achieved, leading to numerous translations.

It is a careful balancing act and a tremendous amount of work to publish a new translation. Some translations attempt a word-for-word translation, which can create an awkward text and hamper clarity. Others forego accuracy to emphasize the literary quality of the text. Still others resort to paraphrasing in hopes of making the text accessible to new or young readers, or even to disrupt the familiar and prompt fresh consideration of the meaning of the text, again threatening the accuracy of the translation. In the end, depending on our point of view, we are either pleased or frustrated by the multitude of translations. I tend toward the former, for each translation makes a contribution toward a more complete understanding.

There are several aspects to consider when selecting a translation of the Bible for yourself. Are you looking for a Bible worthy of academic study, in which case accuracy of translation is of paramount importance, or a more devotional one that may have used paraphrasing? Most of the information you need in order to understand the differences in the translations is readily found in the few pages of preface in the Bibles. Note what organization or group of people sponsored the translation. This will give you clues as to how ecumenical the translation will be, as well as the theological perspective of the translation. The specific translators' names will be included. These translators should have extensive credentials in the biblical languages of Hebrew, Greek, and Aramaic as well as extensive knowledge of the history and culture of the era in which the biblical texts were written. It goes without saying that they should also have an excellent grasp of the target language (English) and culture (American vs. British). Consider how much peer review was given to the translation before it was published. Attention should also be given to the textual basis for the translation. On a more personal note, select a Bible that demonstrates a comfortable grade level of the English language. The explosion of English translations can make the choice seem overwhelming, but by asking a few questions, you can find a translation that comfortably fits your needs.

Reading the Bible

There is also an abundance of valuable resources available today to supplement reading the Bible. Whether you are wanting to dig deeper into scripture, need a jump start to begin, or need a boost to keep reading, there are aids of various forms available.

One of the most useful is a Bible atlas. These atlases map the geographic area where the biblical events took place, showing geopolitical boundaries at various stages during biblical history. They often include overlays of today's geopolitical boundaries of the same lands along with relevant archeological evidence. Also useful is a Bible concordance for your version of the Bible. It will list biblical words alphabetically and indicate the passage(s) where that word can be found. Many study Bibles will contain both an atlas and concordance in abbreviated forms and will additionally include other helpful features, such as variant readings listed in footnotes, articles relating contextual settings such as culture and customs, and annotations explaining difficult passages.

More extensive aids are commentaries. These books help with interpreting the biblical text for what it meant in the time it was written and what it means for us today. Commentaries may take the form of a single volume to cover the entire Bible or a set of volumes, each covering one book of the Bible. They usually give background information as to the author, history, date, and theme of the particular biblical book before providing interpretation of the text either in sections or verse by verse. These series are written at all levels from highly accessible (*Old/New Testament for Everyone* and *The New Interpreter's Bible*), to those which require knowledge of the biblical languages of Hebrew, Aramaic, and Greek (*Word Bible Commentary*) and to those comfortably in between (*New International Biblical Commentary* and *New International Commentary on the New/Old Testament*).

I would also like to mention a few other aids for reading the Bible. There are several schedules for reading the Bible in a year. These usually include reading portions from the Old and New Testament simultaneously. One often starts reading on New Year's with the resolve that this will be the year to read the entire Bible. For those who may get bogged down when attempting to read the entire Bible for the first time, you may appreciate some help to see the bigger picture in order to get over the hump. For that, I recommend *A Reader's Guide to the Bible* by John Goldingay. It is a great read for all levels of Bible students, but especially for any who are not familiar with the entire Bible.

New readers are sometimes encouraged to begin their reading with John's Gospel. It is often put in people's hands at evangelical events, for it contains the familiar theological summary statement found in John 3:16: "For God so loved the world that he gave his only Son, so that everyone who believes in him may not perish but may have eternal life." But I would like to suggest starting with Matthew's Gospel instead. The majority of John's Gospel conveys its message through the literary use of metaphors, imagery, and symbolism. These literary techniques are good mediums to explain or communicate a concept that is beyond our ordinary perception. For example, the symbol points the reader in the direction of its meaning, but the reader must then skillfully and perceptively discern the deeper level of meaning for themselves. A reader that is willing to take the time to unlock the mysteries held within the symbolic narrative of John's Gospel can gain much understanding. But this understanding can be difficult for someone new to the Bible.

It is no accident that Matthew's Gospel is placed first in the New Testament, even though it does not fall first in chronological order. Matthew's thematic ordering, focusing on one new idea at a time, and the concise representation of ideas allows it to be easily read and understood. In addition, the prose is often rhythmic or poetic, such as the group of "blessed are" phrases, making it easily remembered. It gained its place as first in the New Testament because it was the more universally read Gospel in the early churches. Perhaps its popularity was in part because it made use of several common teaching techniques that made it excellent for easy comprehension.

If you have access to a library, browse the religion section and become familiar with all of these and other resources that can complement your Bible reading. Having worked in a library, I can unfortunately just about guarantee you that the religion section will be a quiet and uncrowded oasis in which to study.

Summary

The previous portions of this chapter have provided information that I hope has created an appreciation for the unparalleled uniqueness of the Bible. Against daunting circumstances, the Bible has been preserved over millennia. It has survived the elements of nature, as well as persecution of the Jewish and Christian societies. No less threatening, it has survived controversies from within the very communities that revere it.

We study the Bible because it is the source for what Christians believe. The goal of studying the scriptures is to interpret the meaning of the words in their context. Christian theologian John Goldingay said of insightful study of scripture, "Whether or not we believe in God, we are trying to get inside the thinking of people who did believe in God."[15] We would benefit by understanding the scripture writers' culture and purposes for writing. The beliefs of the Christian faith emerged during the first four centuries AD from this kind of extensive reflection and debate of the biblical source documents.

However, Christians do not always come to the Bible to study it. Following a time of study and interpretation, the Christian, by faith (for it is only by faith that one can trust that the Bible is God's word), may be led to anticipate much more. A myriad of expectations can accompany one as they take their Bibles into their favorite chair to simply read in a devotional way.

When reading in this way, there is an expectation that God will reveal who God is, who we are, and what our purpose is according to God's will. At one reading there may be an expectation of being comforted. On another day, the reader may be challenged by new insights. But because there is an understanding of the hope and love that Christ has made possible, one expects to discover a treasure of God's wisdom with each reading. The most unique aspect of a Christian reading the Bible is the expectation of coming

15. Goldingay, *A Reader's Guide*, 173.

away with treasures which will transform the reader into one who brings more of God's kingdom to earth.

As we read scripture through the lens of Christianity, one can identify with the characters of the Bible stories and thus see oneself from different perspectives. This revelation can prompt an openness to the power of God to transform the reader. It can be an exciting adventure, for one hears not just what one wants to hear, but what God wants to impart. Pick up the Bible and let the text speak.

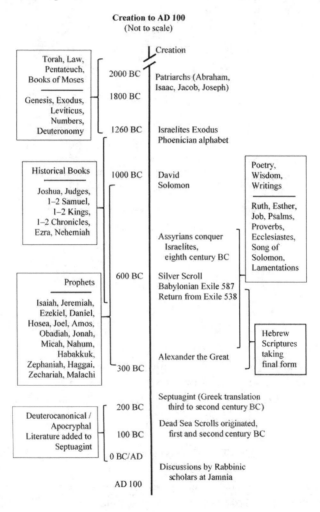

Creation to AD 100
(Not to scale)

Torah, Law, Pentateuch, Books of Moses	2000 BC	Creation
		Patriarchs (Abraham, Isaac, Jacob, Joseph)
Genesis, Exodus, Leviticus, Numbers, Deuteronomy	1800 BC	
	1260 BC	Israelites Exodus Phoenician alphabet
Historical Books	1000 BC	David Solomon
Joshua, Judges, 1–2 Samuel, 1–2 Kings, 1–2 Chronicles, Ezra, Nehemiah		
		Assyrians conquer Israelites, eighth century BC
Prophets	600 BC	Silver Scroll Babylonian Exile 587 Return from Exile 538
Isaiah, Jeremiah, Ezekiel, Daniel, Hosea, Joel, Amos, Obadiah, Jonah, Micah, Nahum, Habakkuk, Zephaniah, Haggai, Zechariah, Malachi	300 BC	Alexander the Great
	200 BC	Septuagint (Greek translation third to second century BC)
Deuterocanonical / Apocryphal Literature added to Septuagint	100 BC	Dead Sea Scrolls originated, first and second century BC
	0 BC/AD	
	AD 100	Discussions by Rabbinic scholars at Jamnia

Poetry, Wisdom, Writings

Ruth, Esther, Job, Psalms, Proverbs, Ecclesiastes, Song of Solomon, Lamentations

Hebrew Scriptures taking final form

AD 0–400
(Not to scale)

AD 50 — Discussions by Rabbinic Scholars at Jamnia

Books of the
New Testament
Written

AD 100 — Clement, Pope of Rome, First Apostolic Father

Ignatius (c. 35–107), Bishop of Antioch, Old
Testament was his Bible

Collection of
Paul's Letters
Circulating,
Early Second
Century

Polycarp (c. 69–155) Bishop of Smyrna, begins
to limit which writings were *authorized*

Papias (c. 60–130) Bishop of Hierapolis, end of
dependence on oral transmission of tradition

AD 125 — Oldest existing New Testament fragment

Marcion (c. 100–160), his heretical bible
accelerated the canonization process

Rule of Faith
Circulating During — AD 150
Second Century

AD 175 — Melito, Bishop of Sardis, First Christian list
of Hebrew Scriptures (c. 170)

Irenaeus (c. 130–200), *Against Heresies*

Nag Hammadi — AD 200 — Tertullian (160–225), challenged Marcion
Library Originated — and Gnostics

Muratorian Document originated

Latin
Replacing — Origen (185–254), Biblical Scholar
Greek

Eusebius (c. 260–340), Bishop of Caesarea

AD 300

Codex Sinaiticus — Athanasius (c. 296–373), Bishop of Alexandria,
first use of the word canon
and first list of 27 NT books

Codex Vaticanus — Augustine, Bishop of Hippo (354–430), listed
books canonized at Council of Carthage

Third Council of Carthage,
AD 400 — Established Canon, 397

Jerome (c. 347–420),
Latin Translation (Vulgate) 405

AD 500–2000
(Not to scale)

AD 500

Masoretes, Copied and Preserved Hebrew
Scriptures (Masoretic Text)

AD 1000

Codex Leningrad

Chapter Numbers
Added to Scripture
Thirteenth Century

AD 1300

Printing Press in use

AD 1500

Martin Luther, Father of Protestant Reformation

Texus Receptus, 1535

Verse Numbers
Added to Scripture
Sixteenth Century

Council of Trent, 1546, Ratified Vulgate

AD 1600

King James Version (KJV) published, 1611

AD 1700

Muratorian Document Discovered, 1740

AD 1900

American Standard Version (ASV), 1901

Dead Sea Scrolls Discovered, 1946

Nag Hammadi Library Discovered, 1947

Revised Standard Version (RSV), 1952

New International Version (NIV), 1984

New Revised Standard Version (NRSV), 1989

AD 2000

Common English Bible (CEB), 2011

3

Doctrine: What Does It Encompass?

WHAT IS DOCTRINE? THE definition is simple enough. Doctrine is the body of Christian beliefs which define the faith and are taught and accepted as true by the church.[1] But this rather straightforward statement invariably sparks more questions. Who determines what beliefs are true? What is the basis for these beliefs? When and where did these beliefs originate? And perhaps the most intriguing question is what beliefs actually fall into this category of doctrine? These are some of the main questions regarding Christian doctrine.

While the apostles were still alive, these eyewitnesses of Jesus' life, death, and resurrection were considered to be the source of knowledge for understanding the doctrines of the faith and the gospel message. Their preaching and writings, which were delivered to emerging Christian communities, articulated the Christian faith and were the means of instructing the people on how these beliefs were to influence their lives. After the apostles were gone, the writings they left behind ultimately became authoritative as the New Testament and were the primary source for understanding the faith. The apostles' writings have also left us evidence that misrepresentations of Christian beliefs would be nothing new. The following scriptural excerpts, written by the apostles to the developing faith communities, demonstrate that false teachers flourished from the beginning.

---

1. I am using the term "doctrine" in the Protestant sense, which is essentially equivalent to the Roman Catholic and Eastern Orthodox use of "dogma." Dogmas in Catholic and Orthodox churches are their officially accepted teachings.

> But false prophets also arose among the people, just as there will be false teachers among you, who will secretly bring in destructive opinions. They will even deny the Master and because of these teachers the way of truth will be maligned. (2 Pet 2:1a, 2b)

> I urge you, as I did when I was on my way to Macedonia, to remain in Ephesus so that you may instruct certain people not to teach any different doctrine, and not to occupy themselves with myths and endless genealogies that promote speculations rather than the divine training that is known by faith. (1 Tim 1:3–4)

This problem of false teaching made for a messy process in defining doctrine. As we retrace the composition of doctrinal statements you may want to refer to the timeline at the end of this chapter.

After the death of the apostles, and before their writings were collected and authorized into scripture, various doctrinal interpretations were promoted. It was a long road to establish a unified orthodox faith—sorting truth from heresy. Factions developed early and the unity of the young faith and church was threatened. Late in the first century, and into the second century and beyond, a number of bishops and theologians composed essays on Christian theology. It was a tumultuous and critical time for Christianity. The early doctrinal disputes would have to be settled without the benefit of the eyewitness apostles, without an official agreed-upon collection of their writings as scripture, and all the while experiencing persecution by the empire. These early theologians were fielding questions that could not be outrightly answered from the apostles' writings. The answers would need to be attained by staying as close as possible to the source of Jesus' and the apostles' teachings, as well as those in direct line of receiving these teachings. Irenaeus (c. 130–200), bishop of Lyons, and others had great confidence that the fledging church communities had received and preserved the true apostolic teaching, since they were birthed by the apostles themselves.[2] Therefore, the *truth* was considered to be found in the writings that would later become collected into the scriptures and the apostolic teachings passed down through these church communities. However, this claim only defines the *sources* of truth for Christians and there was still room for competing interpretations. Irenaeus was aware that even though he could quote from the apostles' writings in support of his doctrinal interpretations, Gnostics could likewise put forth the same writings to support their heretical teachings.[3] However, when Irenaeus convincingly combined interpretations from the writings with the teachings that were left with the initial churches, the

---

2. Roberts and Donaldson, *Saint Irenaeus: Against Heresies*, IV 33.8, 467.
3. Hinson, *Understandings of the Church*, 10.

Gnostic teachings were exposed as heresies. The result of this controversy was that Gnosticism, along with other heresies, gave rise to the need to define the orthodox doctrine of the Christian faith.

Two of the doctrines that created the most debate were at the same time the most critical to the faith. One of these controversies centered around the relation of the divine and the human in Jesus Christ. The other revolved around relations among the tripart but monotheistic Godhead: Father, Son, and Holy Spirit. The endeavors surrounding these debates are often referred to as the Christological and Trinitarian controversies. Tracing these and other controversies of the late first to the fourth centuries is crucial to understanding the formation of Christian doctrines. One of the results of unscrambling these and earlier controversies was the fine-tuning of the Christian creeds. Creeds express the content of the faith with brevity and clarity. Therefore, one way to trace the formation of Christian doctrines is to trace the formation of the creeds. As we will later see, however, the above controversies were not the first situation to set the development of the Christian creeds in motion.

Christian Creeds of the Church

What the creeds became was a succinct and intelligible way to grasp Christian doctrine, making the faith more comprehensible and able to influence and direct the Christian's life. Even though there are no fully developed creedal statements in what became the New Testament, the elements for composing them were contained throughout the apostles' writings.[4] For example, 1 Corinthians 15:1–34 reminds the people, in summary fashion, of Christ's death and resurrection and the significance this has for their lives. Philippians 2:11 simply states, "And every tongue should confess that Jesus Christ is Lord, to the glory of God the Father." Creeds became tools for codifying doctrine and communicating the faith in a consistent manner. But while they lucidly disseminate the faith, creeds are not a substitute for discerning the faith from the scriptures, which continue to have supremacy.

As already implied, creeds originated and were crystallized out of needs that arose within the church. One of those needs was disseminating the faith to new converts. Many of the people entering the churches were from tribal religions; some had no religious background at all. They were unfamiliar with Jewish teachings that carried into Christianity and uninformed of the moral lifestyle this entailed. The first need that prompted the formation of the creeds was for a declaration of beliefs which a potential

4. Kelly, *Early Christian Creeds*, 23–24.

candidate for baptism would be expected to understand and adopt. In the time of the apostles when new converts were baptized, they simply pledged to live according to the faith. As Acts 2:38 says, "Repent, and be baptized every one of you in the name of Jesus Christ so that your sins may be forgiven; and you will receive the gift of the Holy Spirit." This and other short statements were full of meaning. But in the late first and early second century, without eyewitnesses of the faith available for clarification, a need for a comprehensive baptismal confession became necessary.

An early church document, the *Didache*, composed sometime between AD 85 and 150, gives us a picture of the extensive instruction given to those preparing for baptism.[5] This instruction begins with "first: you will love the God who made you; second; your neighbor as yourself," and continues with moral and ethical instructions such as "pray for your enemies . . . you will not murder . . . you will not bear false witness . . . you will not practice magic."[6] And perhaps speaking more directly to the background of many who were receiving this instruction are the words, "Do not become a diviner, since this is the path leading to idolatry; nor an enchanter, nor an astrologer, nor a purifier, nor even wish to see these things, for, from all these, idolatry is begotten."[7]

A standard form developed for including new Christians into the churches. First, they were provided instruction such as we see in the *Didache* and then, at the time of baptism, the candidate would pledge a confession of faith by reciting or by answering questions of the faith.[8] Initially this pledge would likely include renouncing heresies, but later the confession became simply a statement of faith—a creed. In summary, creeds were initially developed as baptismal confessions of faith, but they also satisfied some of the educational needs of the church and were used to halt the spread of heresies. During the second and third centuries creeds proliferated as the local churches each required a declaratory statement for baptismal purposes.[9] Early on they were loosely worded, but by the middle of the third century they became more precise, able to discard heresies simply by stating the faith in unambiguous terms.[10] Eventually, the phraseology became more settled and one creed began to out-compete all the others. It is known as the Old Roman Symbol. Over the years, this creed was expanded and became

5. Patzia and Petrotta, *Pocket Dictionary of Biblical Studies*, 36.

6. Milavec, *The Didache*, 3–15.

7. Milavec, *The Didache*, 9.

8. Kelly, *Early Christian Creeds*, 100.

9. Kelly, *Early Christian Creeds*, 94.

10. Kelly, *Early Christian Creeds*, 98.

the Apostles' Creed. The Nicene Creed has also had a substantial influence and place in the history of the declaration of Christian doctrines. These are the creeds that will inform our study.

Old Roman Symbol

We begin with the earliest of these creeds—the Old Roman Symbol. Through historians' consolidation of fragments of information, there is general consensus that this creed originated between AD 150 and 175 and was first written while the language of Rome was Greek.[11] One of the most explicit sources regarding the Old Roman Symbol comes to us from the Latin writings of Tyrannius Rufinus of AD 404.[12] The italics in this English translation indicate those phrases thought to be later additions.

> I believe in God the Father almighty;
> And in Christ Jesus His *only* Son, *our Lord*, Who was born from *the Holy Spirit and* the Virgin Mary, Who under Pontius Pilate was crucified and buried, on the third day rose again from the dead, ascended to heaven, sits at the right hand of the Father, whence He will come to judge the living and the dead;
> and in the Holy Spirit, *the holy Church, the remission of sins*, the resurrection of the flesh.[13]

Like all creeds, the Old Roman Symbol is believed to have first served as a baptismal confession. Rufinus's confession of baptism was in fact the above version which he believed "retained the apostolic wording intact."[14] Evidence of this creed also appeared in the writings of theologians Irenaeus (c. 130–200) and Tertullian (c.160–220).[15] Its importance is ensconced in the fact that it became a recognizable standard creed, providing unity of beliefs among the local churches in the West and having some influence in the Eastern churches as well. Its development shows signs of a more fully defined Christology, recognizing both Jesus' humanity and divinity. The additions were not seen as departures from the apostolic teachings, but as more complete expressions of these teachings. This creed, however, is most noteworthy because its mature form became the Apostles' Creed.

11. McGiffert, *The Apostles' Creed*, 6–7.
12. Kelly, *Early Christian Creeds*, 102.
13. McGiffert, *The Apostles' Creed*, 6–7.
14. Kelly, *Early Christian Creeds*, 107.
15. McGiffert, *The Apostles' Creed*, 6.

Apostles' Creed

The importance of the Apostles' Creed as a doctrinal norm within all of Western Christianity, and its early influence in the Eastern church, cannot be overstated. Its longevity is without precedence as it is an extension of the Old Roman Symbol whose origin was late in the first century. As with other creeds, its primary role began as a declaration of beliefs at baptism. In the late sixth or early seventh century, when local variations of the wording ceased, this final form of the Old Roman Symbol became what we know as the Apostles' Creed.[16] Below is an English translation of a Latin text from the late middle ages, which is virtually identical to the form used today.

> I believe in God the Father almighty, creator of heaven and earth;
> And in Jesus Christ, His only Son, our Lord, Who was conceived by the Holy Spirit, born from the Virgin Mary, suffered under Pontius Pilate, was crucified, dead and buried, descended to hell, on the third day rose again from the dead, ascended to heaven, sits at the right hand of God the Father almighty, thence He will come to judge the living and the dead;
> I believe in the Holy Spirit, the holy Catholic Church, the communion of saints, the remission of sins, the resurrection of the flesh, and eternal life. Amen.[17]

As a side note, the name now attached to it, Apostles' Creed, was the result of a legend that the creed was composed of twelve statements, with each one coming from one of the twelve apostles. This legend, which was taken seriously for some time, demonstrates how important it was to establish that Christian doctrines adhered to Jesus' and the apostles' original teachings.

We need to take a look at a few of the differences between the Old Roman Symbol and its final form as the Apostles' Creed and determine why the changes might have been added. The first notable addition to the Apostles' Creed is *creator of heaven and earth*. Phrases like this already existed in Eastern local creeds, and it was only a small step to include it in this Western creed. Inclusion of this concept was important because God, as creator of everything, material and spiritual, set the Christian faith apart from other tribal religions.

The new wording *conceived by the Holy Spirit, born from the Virgin Mary* is an indication of a more developed Christology that reveals Jesus' divine and human attributes. His divinity is indicated by the Holy Spirit's

---

16. Kelly, *Early Christian Creeds*, 398–99.
17. Kelly, *Early Christian Creeds*, 369.

action in conception and his humanity by being born of Mary. These words also develop the nuances of the Trinity. With the action of the Holy Spirit being included in the incarnation of Jesus (that is, God coming to earth in human form) the Godhead is now more precisely revealed as including God the Father, Son, and Holy Spirit.

The addition of the holy *catholic* church is a development that recognizes the universal nature of the church, bringing the church together under one umbrella. We will see this concept in action, as ecumenical councils were instrumental in the development of the Nicene Creed. With this addition, along with the addition of the *communion of saints*, the recognition of the unity of Christianity is given voice. Everyone who proclaims Jesus as Christ and Lord makes up the holy *catholic* church and counted in the *communion of saints*. The phrase, *communion of saints*, further embraces a spiritual union of Christians of all the ages, past and present.

The last addition we will look at is the closing words of the creed—the belief in *eternal life*. It is thought this change was added to clarify that references to eternal life are not speaking of bodily life. There was an awareness of the miracle of Jesus raising Lazarus (John 11:1–44) that was creating confusion. Therefore, a distinction needed to be made that the life Jesus ushers in is not bodily life, but rather an attribute or quality of life that is eternal. In current usage of the creed, this is often stated as *life everlasting*. The implication of eternal life is two-fold. First, the Christian life includes a spiritual dimension which begins on earth, and second, this part of life does not end after bodily death but continues eternally.

As we are beginning to see, the creeds are where we catch sight of and follow the refinement and clarification of Christian doctrines. Although these doctrinal statements were initially a baptismal confession, they began to be used for more than that. They were also being regularly recited and used for liturgical purposes. In AD 665 St. Fructuosus, archbishop of Braga, instructed the brethren to "with a united voice recite the symbol of the Christian faith" in their nightly prayers.[18] Documents reveal the symbol they recited to be the Apostles' Creed.[19]

When we look to the practical side of the spread and use of the Apostles' Creed, we must turn to the extensive political influence of Charlemagne (742–814). Charlemagne, also known as Charles I, ruled much of Western Europe for almost half a century, from 768 until his death in 814. His genuine Christian faith led him to launch reforms in the church, including liturgical uniformity and improvement to the theological education of both clergy

18. Kelly, *Early Christian Creeds*, 370–71.
19. Kelly, *Early Christian Creeds*, 370–71.

and laity.[20] During his reign we see two direct influences his faith had on the Apostles' Creed. First, it was made the sole baptismal creed throughout his lands, thus allowing a rapid spread throughout Western Europe. It also gained another purpose. In Charlemagne's efforts to improve the clergy's theological understandings, the bishops were instructed to examine the clergy during Lent of each year on their knowledge of the creed.[21] Further, Charlemagne required the clergy to preach on the creed.[22] This creed was being used as a test of the clergy's orthodox beliefs, a usage that was first seen with the Nicene Creed in the fourth century.

Moving to the furthest reaches of Charlemagne's territories, we make our way to Rome, where Charlemagne added to his kingdom titles and was crowned emperor of the Romans in the year 800. It appears that Charlemagne's presence extended the use of the Apostles' Creed into Rome in the ninth century. However, before the Apostles' Creed reached this region, the Nicene Creed already held the place of prominence. So, we go back in time and pick up the history of the Nicene Creed.

Nicene Creed

A political situation propelled the development of the Nicene Creed. Persecution of Christians was in full force at the beginning of the fourth century. However, Emperor Constantine experienced a vision and dramatic revelation in the year 312 which caused him to reverse his position on Christianity. Not only did Constantine abolish persecution of the Christians, he took an active interest in Christianity and the activities of the church. It will forever be debated whether he did this out of true Christian devotion or political necessity to unite his empire, but the results cannot be denied.

However, the stabilizing influence that Constantine hoped Christianity would provide his empire was at risk because Christianity itself was experiencing discord. The divisiveness centered on the separation of orthodoxy from heresy concerning the understanding of the nature of Jesus Christ. Constantine knew that before Christianity could affect calm within the empire, it must quell its own conflicts. Therefore, in the year 325 Constantine convened the first ecumenical council in Christian history. Over three hundred bishops were assembled, mostly from the Roman empire, but there were representatives from the East as well.[23] Constantine wanted the

20. Latourette, *History of Christianity*, 355–57.

21. Kelly, *Early Christian Creeds*, 422.

22. Latourette, *History of Christianity*, 356.

23. Latourette, *History of Christianity*, 154.

outcome of this meeting to be a consensus on the divisive doctrinal issues. He presided over the meeting himself, which became known as the Council of Nicaea and resulted in the Nicene Creed of 325, a precursor to, but not the same as, the Nicene Creed used in churches today.

We will return to the historical background momentarily, but at this point we can look at the doctrinal issue that was causing such discord. The departure from orthodoxy was promoted by Arius (c. 256–336), a theologian from Alexandria, Egypt. Arius did not believe Jesus to be fully divine. Although he believed Jesus to be the highest created being of God, he placed Jesus subordinate to God. These thoughts went against the orthodox doctrine of the Trinity, as well as the orthodox doctrine of Jesus Christ's identity. The question the debate came down to was: "Is the Logos [Jesus] God in the same way that the Father is God?"[24] The council answered this question in the affirmative, and Arius's ideas were declared heresy. It should be noted that the council was not covering totally new ground. Tertullian (160–220) was the first to speak of the Trinity in terms of one substance in three persons, and while Origen (185–254) also expounded orthodox views of the Trinity, he unwittingly laid the groundwork for Arius's claims through his lack of clarity.

As a result of the Council of Nicaea, the creed included words that defined the Son to be *homoousios* with the Father, that is, they share the same substance. Jesus is divine as well as human, and is not subordinate to the Father, but an equal part of the one triune God. This resolution solved the issue of the day and words reflecting this important nuance were captured in the creed, printed as follows:

> We believe in one God, the almighty, maker of all things visible and invisible;
> And in one Lord Jesus Christ, the Son of God, begotten from the Father, only-begotten, that is, from the substance of the Father, God from God, light from light, true God from true God, begotten not made, of one substance with the Father, through Whom all things came into being, things in heaven and things on earth, Who because of us men and because of our salvation came down and became incarnate, becoming man, suffered and rose again on the third day, ascended to the heavens, will come to judge the living and the dead;
> And in the Holy Spirit.
> But as for those who say, There was when He was not, and, Before being born He was not, and that He came into existence out of nothing, or who assert that the Son of God is of a different

24. Olson, *Pocket History of Theology*, 31.

hypostasis or substance, or is subject to alteration or change—
these the Catholic and apostolic Church anathematizes.[25]

This Nicene Creed of 325 contained more than just words putting to rest the Arian heresy; it was a full creedal statement. The base creed was probably a local region's baptismal creed, brought to the council by one of the bishops in attendance. Its choice of wording appeared to most likely be of Syrian or Palestinian origin.[26]

The anti-Arian words tacked onto the end of the creed were significant. They indicate the church anathematized, that is, excommunicated, those who still held to Arius's heresy. This was the beginning of using the statements of faith as tests of one's orthodoxy. Bishops were asked to sign the creed, showing their agreement with it, and those who refused, such as Arius, were exiled. This creed was much more of a bishop's creed than a baptismal creed, with its distinctions of the orthodox faith and inclusion of harsh warnings.[27] Therefore, the local variations of the Old Roman Symbol continued to be favored as the baptismal creed. This Nicene Creed remained the accepted orthodoxy until the Council of Constantinople in 381. At that time the full Trinity was addressed, adding belief in the Holy Spirit as part of the Godhead, officially condemning Arianism and recognizing the full humanity, as well as full divinity, of Jesus. The result of this council was the Niceno-Constantinopolitan Creed, as it appears below:

> We believe in one God, the Father, almighty, maker of heaven and earth, of all things visible and invisible;
>
> And in one Lord Jesus Christ, the only begotten Son of God, begotten from the Father before all ages, light from light, true God from true God, begotten not made, of one substance with the Father, through Whom all things came into existence, Who because of us men and because of our salvation came down from heaven, and was incarnate from the Holy Spirit and the Virgin Mary and became man, and was crucified for us under Pontius Pilate, and suffered and was buried, and rose again on the third day according to the Scriptures and ascended to heaven, and sits on the right hand of the Father, and will come again with glory to judge living and dead, of Whose kingdom there will be no end;
>
> And in the Holy Spirit, the Lord and life-giver, Who proceeds from the Father, Who with the Father and the Son is

25. Kelly, *Early Christian Creeds*, 215–16.
26. Kelly, *Early Christian Creeds*, 227.
27. Kelly, *Early Christian Creeds*, 255.

together worshipped and together glorified, Who spoke through the prophets; in one holy Catholic and apostolic Church. We confess one baptism to the remission of sins; we look forward to the resurrection of the dead and the life of the world to come. Amen.[28]

The next significant discussion of orthodox doctrine came in 451 at the Council of Chalcedon, attended by close to five hundred bishops and numerous state officials. This council did not result in a change to the creed, but produced a statement, known as the Chalcedon Formula. This statement is an elaboration of the creed in that it sets boundaries for defining the relationship between Jesus Christ's humanity and divinity and is the orthodox statement on the person of Christ. It reads in part:

> . . . our Lord Jesus Christ is . . . made known in two natures without confusion, without change, without division, without separation; the difference of the natures being by no means removed because of the union but the property of each nature being preserved and coalescing in one person . . . [29]

Emergence of Contention

As we can now see, the role of defining doctrine was embraced by the bishops and theologians of the church, with some legitimizing by imperial state officials, and took the form of being expressed in creeds. Through the trek of the early Christian centuries and up to the AD 451 ecumenical Council of Chalcedon, the bishops of the Eastern and Western churches were colleagues and in theological agreement.

However, a threat to this unity began to take shape in the ninth and tenth centuries. The office of the bishop of Rome was beginning to define itself as having authority over all of Christendom. The East understood their own bishops to be equal among themselves and equal colleagues with bishops of the West. Then around 850 the Eastern Constantinople church discovered that the Latin term *filioque*, which translates as *and the Son*, was inserted in the Niceno-Constantinopolitan Creed by the Western church without their knowledge. The process of exactly how the Western church added this clause is uncertain. It read as follows (for clarity the *filioque* clause is italicized).

28. Kelly, *Early Christian Creeds*, 297–98.
29. Olson, *Pocket History of Theology*, 48–49.

> We believe . . . in the Holy Spirit, the Lord and life-giver, Who
> proceeds from the Father *and the Son*, Who with the Father and
> the Son is together worshipped and together glorified.[30]

The East resisted the West's seizure of authority and this discord reached a boiling point in 1054. The Eastern church's objection to the additional clause was on two fronts. First, the ecumenical Niceno-Constantinopolitan Creed that was previously agreed upon had been altered by the West without their consultation or approval. The second and more profound reason concerned the theology of the Trinity. The root of the theological problem was the issue of where the Holy Spirit derived its being. Was it from the Father, or from the Father *and the Son*? In 1054 the two churches each accused the other of heresy and excommunicated each other. The rift remains unhealed, but less contentious, to this day. Both the Roman Catholics and Eastern Orthodox claim to be the owner of orthodoxy and have continued in their distinctive understandings. Now is a good time to note that the text of the Niceno-Constantinopolitan Creed with the added clause is currently used by the Roman Catholic and Protestant churches. However, it is known by its reprised name—the Nicene Creed.

From a doctrinal perspective, another significant rift reached its climax in the sixteenth century. This fracture again brushed up against the Roman Catholic Church and its self-proclaimed authority within Christendom. The protestors, who became the Protestants, challenged the church's authority, claiming that the ultimate authority is the Holy Spirit speaking through the scriptures, not the church. These reformers claimed the Roman Catholic Church was departing from the teachings which the apostles and the early church fathers set forth. The most visible example of the church drifting off course was their collection of indulgences. These financial contributions were said to pay for the removal of guilt and punishment for sin and could also ensure the person a swift path to heaven when they died. The protesters, particularly Martin Luther (1483–1546) could find no scriptural validation for this practice. However, the indulgences were only the visible symptom of a theological issue concerning a fundamental doctrine. It concerned God's work of salvation through Jesus Christ. Chapter 5 takes a comprehensive look at the meaning of salvation, but for now, we can define it as God's work through Jesus Christ to restore contrite sinners to fullness of life and the world to its intended glory. Luther's point was that the saving work of Christ and remission of sin is God's work. It is not achieved by the payments or mandates which the church required of the people. Luther's understanding of the doctrine of salvation included the belief that a person's

---

30. Kelly, *Early Christian Creeds*, 358.

salvation is solely dependent on their faith in Jesus Christ's saving work at his resurrection. There are no human works or efforts of any kind (particularly paying indulgences) other than faith that merit this grace given by God. Luther's stand was reminiscent of Athanasius's (c. 296–373) reason for fighting against Arianism (the heresy that Jesus was not fully God). Both concerned salvation. Athanasius held to the core of the gospel message that only God can grant remission of sins, therefore for Jesus Christ to open the door to salvation he must be of the same essence as the Father, fully divine.

Martin Luther was only one of the outspoken leaders and contributors of this period of reformation which encompassed the sixteenth to seventeenth centuries. The resulting outcome was the departure from the Roman Catholic Church of those who took exception to their practices. This drove the birth of Protestant churches, with each holding to their distinct theological reflections. The issue of diversity within the Protestant churches will be further addressed in chapter 4.

We would like to think that there is a single, fully defining doctrinal statement that is agreed upon by every Christian. However, the reality is that we do not have complete unity within Christendom. There have been two major rifts that are still unhealed, and at their core they divide us on major aspects of the faith. The AD 1054 schism between the Eastern and Western churches introduced disparity in understanding the internal relationships between the Father, Son, and Holy Spirit. The Protestant Reformation of the sixteenth century introduced disparity in our understanding of the relation of God to humanity to bring about salvation. These two variances illustrate that there are still problems whose solution eludes us. We as theologians continue to listen for revelation from the scriptures and the Holy Spirit to make known to us the mysteries of our faith. The reflection on scripture, which guides doctrinal creeds, is ongoing, but the altering of a creed is not taken lightly.

The major branches of Christianity—Roman Catholicism, Eastern Orthodoxy, and Protestantism—and the offshoots of these three all strive to understand and preserve the teachings of the apostles and early church fathers. This theological task continues to find ways to intelligibly express doctrine for each contemporary generation. However, even as new creeds continue to be written, the Apostles' and Nicene Creeds remain the closest expression of a worldwide unified doctrinal statement as we are likely to find. These two creeds continue to serve diverse situations of church life, including baptismal confessions, instructional documents for potential followers of Christ, tests for orthodox vs. heretical beliefs, and liturgical elements of worship services.

Social Principles

We must now address the fact that the creeds are incomplete as an expression of the whole gospel message. The doctrinal creeds speak to the foundational beliefs Christians share, but they do not speak to the living out of those beliefs. For example, while the creeds acknowledge the redemptive nature of salvation, they do not fully expound how salvation is received by the individual. To implement the complete message of the Gospels we must move beyond doctrine into interpretive areas. While clarity of our beliefs is certainly necessary before we can embark on defining right living, additional interpretation is necessary to determine appropriate actions in various situations. A further demonstration of the incompleteness of doctrinal creeds is the omission of Jesus' teachings such as the great commandments:

> "You shall love the Lord your God with all your heart, and with all your soul, and with all you mind." This is the greatest and first commandment. And a second is like it: "You shall love your neighbor as yourself." (Matt 22:37b–39)

Many of Jesus' teachings were devoted to living out a life of love and justice. In response, some churches have compiled social principle statements which guide their congregations toward their understanding of good moral actions. They are not doctrinal statements, but rather statements of social principles that define what is right and good in regard to particular issues. They are intended to be general rules of conduct that broadly engage the essential elements of the matter. While these statements dispensed by the churches are informed by scripture, they often hinge on situations or technologies that did not exist when the Bible was penned and must now be examined in the light of not only scripture, but also our expanding knowledge of the world. Some of the early statements dealt with the issues of slavery. Examples of current issues include race relations, issues of war and peace, human sexuality, abortion, care of the planet, genetic technologies, end-of-life medical decisions, global economic systems, and gender equality. Emotions can run high over these controversial topics, and impassioned feelings can tempt people to elevate their interpretation of what is right and good into Christian doctrine.

In the New Testament Jesus' teachings often led to an understanding of *right conduct* in particular situations, as did Paul's preaching and teaching. This term, *right conduct*, is the crucial aspect of morality. A good definition of morality is the "dimension of life related to right conduct, including virtuous character, honorable intentions, and right actions."[31] Moral principles

31. Clark and Rakestraw, *Readings in Christian Ethics*, 313.

regarding right and wrong can be ascertained by individuals or by groups, as in the case of the church's summarized statements of social principles. When moralizing, whether it be individuals or the church, it is always good to keep in mind the instructions given in Micah 6:8, namely, to do justice, and to love kindness, and to walk humbly with God.

Individuals, as with the church, do the best they can in searching the scriptures. Theologian Richard Longenecker summarized four ways Christians use the scriptures when making ethical decisions.[32] While he does not recommend exclusive use of any one of the approaches, he concludes that each approach has some value in obtaining truth leading to right conduct. He also outlined the limitations of each. Understanding the approaches taken to form social principles can be helpful, as we are continually faced with moral decisions in our rapidly changing world.

The first approach Longenecker examines is the reading of the scripture as a book of rules and laws. The limitation of this legalistic approach is that the Bible does not contain a rule for every situation, and we are still required to provide an interpretation when new situations in new contexts arise. A second way to read scripture is to look for the underlying principles in biblical situations, and then apply them to our contemporary situations. The caution he gave for this approach is to resist going too far toward philosophy and reason while leaving the moral imperative behind. The third approach is to depend on revelations one receives from the Holy Spirit as one reads the scriptures. While everyone can certainly receive such revelation, and is indeed encouraged to seek such guidance, caution requires that further consultation with the community be considered, for we are all vulnerable to overly subjective and self-serving interpretations of scripture. The fourth way of using scripture to deal with decisions about contemporary ethical issues is to focus on the directive to love one another. After fully investigating a particular situation, one is to choose the most loving action. The difficulty with this approach is that the nature and content of love must still be determined by the individual or group.

Christians who take on the responsibility to condense *right conduct* into social principles or creedal statements have a difficult but important task. As well as searching the scriptures, they must commit to thorough research of the issues in order to be well versed in all sides. Also, in looking for guidance in scripture, it has been well stated that they must "inevitably use some kind of interpretational procedure to determine what the 'then' situation [of the scriptures] says to our 'now' situation."[33] Our lives

---

32. Longenecker, "Four Ways," 185–91.

33. Clark and Rakestraw, *Readings in Christian Ethics*, 182.

are immersed in complicated ethical issues. Social principle statements are helpful guidelines toward reaching agreement or coming to understandings that promote living in harmony. However, these statements do not relieve each of us, individually, from the responsibility of study and reflection on these issues.

Summary

We live with complicated ethical issues, paradoxes of faith, and variances in theological concepts. It is human nature to be uncomfortable with these ambiguities. As individuals, we have a responsibility to consider our beliefs and strive for clarity. The social principle statements and doctrinal creeds of the church are tools that can help us do that.

Struggling with our questions and the mysteries associated with them can be valuable. By exploring questions of morality, we expand our empathy. Likewise, there is value in struggling with doctrinal questions. In that reflective thinking, the merit is found in our expanded engagement with and understanding of God. Doctrinal creeds ground our faith and protect us from self-invented forms of religion. God of course is bigger than our creeds and we cannot fully define God by a creed. But our creeds do have a powerful function. Like stories, they open up a new world of faithful exploration into what we really believe and are the best formulations of what we can never fully grasp. Christians are defined by who they worship, and the doctrinal creeds describe the object of our faith—God the Father, Jesus Christ his Son, and the Holy Spirit. This is the unifying foundation of the Christian faith and the underpinning of any Christian quest.

Timeline—Creed Development

Not to scale

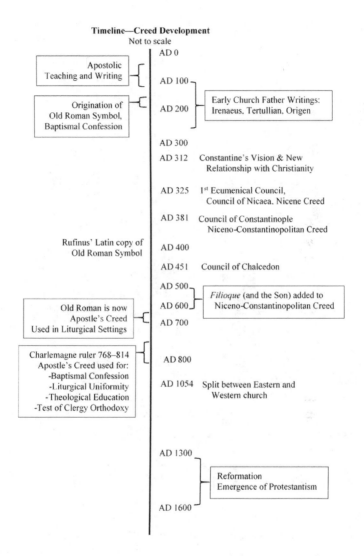

4

Denominations: Are There Versions of Christianity?

THE NUMBER OF CHRISTIAN denominations in North America is estimated to be in the thousands.[1] How did one faith become so splintered? Do all these denominations represent the Christian faith? Does the Bible address this fragmented situation? What caused this explosion of denominations?

As we saw in the previous chapter, variances in the thought and practice of Christianity resulted in three distinct Christian assemblies. The Eastern and Western churches officially separated in 1054 into the Eastern Orthodox and Roman Catholic churches respectively. In the sixteenth century divergence from the Roman Catholic Church led to the formation of major Protestant denominations. Martin Luther began the basis for Lutheranism with the posting of his ninety-five theses; John Calvin and Ulrich Zwingli introduced reformed theology which fashioned the Presbyterian church; Menno Simons's reforms ushered in the Mennonites. The Episcopal and Methodist churches emerged in America from the Church of England, which itself had broken with papal authority in the 1530s. With these and other reformers, the explosion of denominations was off and running.

Now, in the twenty-first century, it is difficult to even know the exact number of Protestant denominations.[2] The number is large enough that it would be a formidable task to be informed about all of them. The *Handbook of Denominations in the United States*, now in its fourteenth edition, is

1. Wright, *Paul for Everyone*, 44.

2. A denomination is defined as a group of congregations that recognize some form of affiliation among themselves.

widely regarded as the gold standard of research into the beliefs, statistics, and histories of over two hundred significant denominations.[3] One way to learn about your church, as well as appreciate your neighbors' church, is to explore this reference book. As we investigate the explosion of Protestant denominations in North America, we will *not* look in depth at individual denominations, but rather try to answer the fundamental questions presented above.

Before embarking on the diversity manifest within Christianity, I would like to consider what unifies all Christians. Christian unity emanates from the belief that Jesus Christ is Lord and Savior. This message is consistent in the New Testament, the subsequent doctrinal creeds, and current ecumenical organizations such as the World Council of Churches. Preserving unity among Christians was vital as the gospel message spread and churches quickly sprang up over large geographic regions. We see this concern in the following first-century appeal which encouraged the church in Ephesus to maintain unity. The very existence of this appeal confirms that some kind of diversity was already emerging.

> . . . with all humility and gentleness, with patience, bearing with one another in love, making every effort to maintain the unity of the Spirit in the bond of peace. There is one body and one Spirit . . . one hope . . . one Lord, one faith, one baptism, one God . . . (selected from Eph 4:2–6)

First Century

As we explore the New Testament we will find, from beginning to end, the tenacious unity that centers on Jesus Christ as Lord and Savior. But we will also learn that there were unique situations which forged diversity among the churches. Unity and uniformity are not the same thing. When churches today are troubled with difficult splintering issues, they often lament and long for the way it was in the beginning. They hope to find that the Lord gave one uniform recipe for establishing the church. But that is not what we find in the scriptures, where we discover that the churches' structures, endeavors, and aspirations exemplify much variance. The only consistent model that emerges from studying New Testament churches is, ironically, a need for flexibility to adapt to various circumstances. Each faith community, within their unique setting, sought a true understanding of how to live their lives according to Christ's teaching. Like current denominations, these

3. Olson et al., *Handbook of Denominations*, xxv.

churches may have looked different, but they all held to that one unifying message, and all identify as Christian.

Raymond Brown, a Catholic priest who respected the ecumenical nature of studying scripture, extensively analyzed the churches in the New Testament. He uncovered an abundance of common ground as well as considerable diversity.[4] As we look more closely at the New Testament churches, we will similarly see that *unity* is the intention, but any expectation of *uniformity* is unsupported.

Churches in the New Testament

Representative of the churches in the pastoral epistles, 1 Timothy describes an institutional-style church with a defined leadership structure and established ways of administering the church. It describes the qualifications of bishops, deacons, and elders (1 Tim 3–6). The teaching and preaching of "sound words of our Lord Jesus Christ" (1 Tim 6:3) is their focus. As to the flock, the care of older persons and widows is spelled out in detail (1 Tim 5:1–16). This well-organized hierarchical style may work well in such an established congregation with a stable population but might not work as well in a new missionary field. In the pastorals we find that the churches did not allow any recent converts to hold a leadership position (1 Tim 3:6). This rigid condition would make it difficult to fill positions when establishing a new church, whereas less emphasis on a system of authority would allow for needed flexibility. A church whose population is mobile and in constant flux would also likely benefit from reduced layers of authority.

Another church setting represented in the New Testament accommodates Christians with a contemplative temperament. This style of church fosters a more individualized relationship with Christ. Such a style is represented in the quiet spiritualism exemplified in the Gospel of John. In this setting, the strong leadership that was so important in the pastorals is not as necessary. The structure that serves this church embraces shared accountability rather than a hierarchical design. The Gospel of John reflects a community that acknowledged knowing Christ in a deeply personal way.

> Abide in me as I abide in you. Just as the branch cannot bear fruit by itself unless it abides in the vine, neither can you unless you abide in me. (John 15:4)

> As the Father has loved me, so I have loved you; abide in my love. (John 15:9)

4. Brown, *Churches the Apostles Left*, 29–30.

> But the Advocate, the Holy Spirit, whom the Father will send in my name, will teach you everything, and remind you of all that I have said to you. Peace I leave with you; my peace I give to you. I do not give to you as the world gives. Do not let your hearts be troubled, and do not let them be afraid. (John 14:26–27)

We might describe such a church as having a high Christology and low ecclesiology. That is, the congregations are particularly aware that Jesus Christ is their leader who directs their lives, while they place less emphasis on the affairs of the authoritative figures of the church.

In contrast, the churches at Ephesus and Colossae place an emphasis on the duties entrusted to the church itself. Their focus is more ecclesiological than christological. Even though knowing Christ is at the center of their mission, there is also substantial emphasis placed on the community of believers, or body of Christ, who strive to make their particular talent or God-given gift available to each other and the efforts of the church.

> The gifts he [Christ] gave were that some would be apostles, some prophets, some evangelists, some pastors and teachers, to equip the saints for the work of ministry, for building up the body of Christ. (Eph 4:11–12)

> But speaking the truth in love, we must grow up in every way into him who is the head, unto Christ, from whom the whole body, joined and knit together by every ligament with which it is equipped, as each part is working properly, promotes the body's growth in building itself up in love. (Eph 4:15–16)

The church working together, united in love and staying connected to Christ, is seen as the model that will result in imitating Christ's love, which is the mandate for these churches.

When we move to the book of Acts, we see churches that were spurred into bold mission by means of the Holy Spirit. Numerous examples demonstrate that these churches were dependent on the guidance of the Holy Spirit rather than the support of an organized structure. In Acts 11:28–29 we see the Holy Spirit impart a prophetic message concerning famine that led the disciples to send relief. In Acts 8 the Spirit is directing Philip in spreading the gospel message. In Acts 13:2–4 Barnabas and Paul were directed in their mission by the Holy Spirit. Acts 15:28 credits the Holy Spirit with guiding the Jerusalem Council into a decision that the conservative Jews should stop troubling the Gentiles, thus setting in motion reconciliation among the diverse groups of Christians. Acts 16:6 details the Spirit guiding the direction of Paul's missionary travels, thus determining the path of the spread of the gospel. Through reliance on the power of the Holy Spirit the persons featured in Acts are less associated with a local church and are more representative of missionaries being Christ's witnesses to the universal church.

In addition to the various New Testament church models that have been demonstrated, the places of meeting varied. Some followers initially met in the synagogues, while others met in small house fellowships, and we even find a reference to using the river as a meeting place.

> On the sabbath day we went outside the gate by the river, where we supposed there was a place of prayer; and we sat down and spoke to the women who had gathered there. (Acts 16:13)

The early church also showed flexibility with regard to how they received and recognized a person into Christianity. There were some common elements of reception into the church, such as the expectance of repentance, belief, and baptism. However, there was diversity in how these acts were assessed and administered (Acts 2:38–42, 8:35–38, 19:2–7).

Summing up, there was no normative pattern in the early church. The highly organized and structured churches were seen providing stability and continuity of the gospel message, but they could also be less capable to adapt to new situations. And while the churches that depended on the Holy Spirit to intervene at crucial moments showed a marked ability to respond to new situations, they had to make sure they were hearing God clearly and not being blinded by their own needs to the detriment of the bigger picture of the world. What was important for all of these churches was that they remained true to Christ and carried this tradition forward in a way appropriate to their particular setting. The exact means would take into consideration the cultural situation as well as the temperament, gifts, and needs of the people. The uniqueness of time, place, and need generally determined the nature of a specific church.

Splintering in the New Testament

The first-century churches shared unity of belief in Jesus Christ as Lord and Savior, but they were not necessarily uniform in their practices. This situation persists in our churches today. Also, just like today, churches in the first century suffered some quarrels. We will look at two of these disputes, one concerning a theological issue, and one of a more personal nature. First is the confrontation between Peter and Paul in Antioch, described in Galatians. On the surface it looks like an argument over a trivial matter of table fellowship. But it represented the deeper theological issue of unity and fellowship among all Christians. Peter was a Jewish Christian who had grown up respecting the Jewish food laws. But as a follower of Christ he, like Paul, realized these Jewish laws were not essential to Christianity and did not have to be upheld among Gentile converts. However, Paul discovered that Peter had reverted to upholding the law by not sharing table fellowship with the Gentile Christians. Paul called Peter out on his hypocrisy, sternly reminding the church to manifest the loving and inclusive fellowship to which Christ calls them. Gentile or Jew makes no difference, all who are in Christ belong to the same fellowship.

This squabble between Peter and Paul was not a simple matter of choosing between two acceptable interpretations of whom one sits down at the table with; it threatened the unity of the faithful. The church is in constant motion as it learns what it means to be a follower of Christ and continually makes necessary adjustments to live accordingly. Leaders of the churches, then and now, have the difficult and ongoing task of separating the critical issues that really matter in the life of a Christian from those that are inconsequential. Jews and Gentiles sharing table may have seemed trivial at first, but deeper reflection revealed its seriousness because it was pertinent to the unity and inclusive fellowship which Christ calls us to.

The second splintering, found in Acts 15:36–41, was between Paul and Barnabas and was more of a personal nature. While it concerned two friends rather than the church, it still had consequences to the mission of the church. Paul and Barnabas were preparing to go on a second missionary journey together. Barnabas wanted to take John Mark with them, but Paul did not, believing that John Mark had proven to be unreliable in their first mission. The disagreement was sharp enough that it caused Paul and Barnabas to part ways. They did not make this an issue of who was right and who was wrong; they simply each continued to proceed in the manner that they felt called. Barnabas and Paul, with different temperaments, different spiritual gifts, and different teams, each went his own way. Barnabas, as an encourager, gave John Mark another opportunity and took him on his mission to Cyprus. Paul continued his mission with Silas, strengthening the churches throughout Syria and Cilicia. The end result was two missionary journeys instead of one, thereby increasing the spread of the gospel message. Disagreements between Christians, especially leaders of the churches, do not always have such a satisfactory ending. However, we can be assured that with all our human diversity, differences will on occasion lead to impasses, and there will be a need to seek God's voice for resolutions.

Modern Times

Time does not stand still, and although there is much that can be learned by looking at the first-century churches and the lives of the leaders of long ago, we live in the twenty-first century with its unique set of circumstances. The New Testament churches revealed their natural predisposition to diversity and that they were not without issues of disagreement. As we turn to contemporary times, we will consider how the North American setting is predisposed to a vast number of churches and denominations, as well as some factors that make them susceptible to splintering.

Proliferation of Churches

Constantine in the fourth century and Charlemagne in the eighth were actively involved with the churches in their lands, using Christianity as a means to unite their empires. Even though it was, at least in part, a political strategy, it contributed to the unity (and to a large degree, uniformity) of the church by dictum. In a Muslim country in the 1990s I attended the one and only Protestant church allowed by the government. It was a beautiful experience with people from many Christian denominations around the world worshipping together. It was an experience that I am sure contributes to my ambivalence about the vast number of denominations that have sprung up in the United States. My skepticism regarding the necessity of this many denominations aside, the political situations mentioned above bring to light one of the major explanations why American churches have divided into so many denominations—simply, because they can. The first amendment to the Constitution guarantees this freedom: "Congress shall make no law respecting an establishment of religion, or prohibiting the free exercise thereof."

This law, as it befittingly protects one's religious rights, enabled the introduction and propagation of many ethnic churches which were established as waves of people entered America, bringing with them their unique religious heritages. Among these are the Quakers, who settled in Pennsylvania, and the many Orthodox churches in America, such as Greek, Armenian, Russian, and Ukrainian. Indeed, most of the mainline Protestant denominations were brought to America from overseas. Freedom of religion also allows anyone with a novel or even unconventional idea to launch a new church. Two outcomes of the Reformation encourage this kind of innovative thinking. First it was proclaimed that scripture alone defined the faith, while secondly it was maintained that individuals, not only church authorities, could interpret scripture. When new interpretations of scripture or trends in theology appear, new churches spring up. Such was the case in the 1970s, when Spirit-filled revivals led to many new charismatic churches.

Most denominations are defined and set apart by some unique set of theological ideas. However, a new denomination does not need to ascribe to a new theological trend; a simple difference in theological emphasis has contributed to the founding of many new churches. One theologian reflected that churches can be sorted by which part of the Trinity they emphasize.[5] Another developed this idea a little further, conjecturing that mainline denominations look more to God, the First Person of the Trinity, while evangelicals emphasize Jesus Christ, the Second Person, and Pentecostals look to the presence and activity of the Third Person of the Trinity, the Holy Spirit.[6] This narrowing of the Trinity certainly seems conceivable, even if regrettable, for God has revealed himself to us in multiple ways for multiple purposes. We engage with God, the First Person of the Trinity, as we reflect on creation and how we fit into and contribute to God's greater universal purposes. The Second Person of the Trinity, Jesus Christ, reveals God's engagement with our individual salvation and his greater plan for restoring the world. And the Third Person, the Holy Spirit, directs our hearts and minds for leading and nurturing the community of faith. Although no church focuses solely on one person of the Trinity, they occasionally and unwittingly weight different facets of the triune God by their ministry concentration.

Another development that generates new churches is concentrating on a specific mission field, such as reaching out to those who have never been introduced to a church. Churches can also distinguish themselves by whom they serve. Do they primarily serve their own membership, or do they reach outside their church to those who are in need, or do they use their limited resources to reach areas that have experienced natural disasters? How a community worships can also distinguish a church. Is the style traditional, liturgical, or contemporary? Is worship designed as presentation or participation? New technology has also created the opportunity for media churches that operate completely on the internet. Also emerging are churches designed to attract people with a common special interest, such as cowboy churches. From the above discussion and examples, we observe that the proliferation of churches has largely resulted from some form of specialization. It can entail a theological, organizational, or cultural aspect. But theology, one's belief system, is what forms the foundation and upholds a

---

5. Schaller, *Discontinuity and Hope*, 37.
6. Robinson, *What's Theology*, 66–67.

church. Therefore, theological differences are the critical distinctions which set apart denominations.

Taking a closer look at how a theological position is developed will help demonstrate this primary reason for so many denominations. I need to present some background information before proceeding. I am not comfortable *labeling* anyone's theology, but I will need to use some classifications in order to express the diversity that arises in congregations. Labels can be divisive and are seldom accurate in fully defining a person or congregation's beliefs. However, a theological spectrum is a useful delineation for classifying congregations. The tagging of a congregation or person's belief system as left or right leaning is usually associated with liberal and conservative theologies, respectively. Those without rigid theological boundaries might represent the far left and ultra conservative fundamentalists the far right, with a large spectrum in the middle ground between these extremes, including progressive, liberal, neo-orthodox, evangelical, and conservative. Even if you dislike this way of referring to theological leanings, it will be useful in the following discussion.

We each have a responsibility to examine and identify our beliefs about God, ourselves, and the world. This theological task, as it is often called, will reveal the reason for the existence of so many denominations. This is not only the basis for how so many churches have come into existence but can also demonstrate how splintering of churches occurs. The task begins by recognizing that each person and congregation holds a set of beliefs, with some plainly stated and others more vaguely implied. Stanley Grenz and Roger Olson have expressed that these beliefs, whether one is consciously aware of them or not, can be divided into three categories which can be described in the following way.[7] The first category is Christian *doctrine* or dogma. These beliefs are considered by the church to be essential, and if people do not believe in them it is assumed that they have not accepted the gospel message of Jesus Christ. The second category contains *beliefs* which are not considered essential but are important enough that they determine fellowship among the flock. Without ascribing to these intermediate beliefs, one would probably not be asked to lead or teach within the church. The third category is composed of beliefs that are not thought to be important to the faith and are mere *opinions*. While the faith community may recognize that a person in their community holds a variant opinion from what they counsel, it is considered relatively unimportant as long as it does not contradict a doctrine.

7. Grenz and Olson, *Who Needs Theology*, 73–76.

Having said all this, we now come to the heart of the matter—"different Christian groups populate these categories with different beliefs" and there is "no universal categorization."[8] Aside from the primary Christian doctrinal belief that Jesus Christ is Lord and Savior, which is held alike by Catholic, Orthodox, and Protestant churches, there are an enormous number of beliefs that populate these categories. Grenz and Olson identified that, in general, the churches that land further to the right, toward fundamentalism, place more beliefs into the doctrine category and fewer beliefs into the less restrictive categories. On the other hand, the more left leaning churches tend to place fewer beliefs into the doctrine category and more into the middle and opinion categories.[9] When a new church is planted, the founders usually have a good understanding of their beliefs and how much importance is ascribed to each.

Let us look at some of the beliefs that populate these categories. First, the degree to which scripture is considered authoritative is usually of particular concern. Is it interpreted literally or as an inspirational collection of literature or somewhere in between? Can only the leaders interpret the scriptures, or the individual congregants as well? How one receives salvation is another important area that often exposes variance. Is salvation by faith alone or is there some action that must be performed by the individual? Denominations also differ in which sacraments they uphold and how they are administered. Beliefs can differ concerning the end-times, angels, the demonic, and charismatic gifts such as healing and speaking in tongues. Denominations also differ on how to structure the church, including the process for selecting their leaders and what authority each have.

As you can imagine, there are an almost unlimited number of combinations of beliefs and ways they can be distributed among the three categories of doctrine, belief, and opinion. Each denomination represents one of these combinations. Conversely, each possible combination of beliefs distributed among these categories can represent a different denomination. Perhaps the estimate of thousands of denominations is reasonable after all.

Proliferation via Splintering

Keep this method of categorizing beliefs into doctrine, belief, and opinion in mind as we now look further into how churches splinter. In the 1700s two theologians, John Wesley and George Whitefield, worked closely together, sometimes serving the same communities of faith. In the beginning of their

8. Grenz and Olson, *Who Needs Theology*, 73–74.
9. Grenz and Olson, *Who Needs Theology*, 77.

joint ministries their theological concepts were similar, and similarly distributed among the categories. However, as time went on, they began to differ in their understanding of the attainment of an individual's salvation. The Calvinist view of predestination eventually became an essential doctrine of Whitefield's theology of salvation, but Wesley considered predestination blasphemy.[10] They obviously now populated their belief categories differently. In time, their theological reflections ended up being represented in two distinct denominations. Whitefield's views on predestination can today be found in the Presbyterian Church, while Wesley was one of the founders of the Methodist Church. The people they served divided; the faith community was split.

When situations change, new leaders emerge or new visions develop, and beliefs are moved from one category to another (such as taking a mere opinion and moving it into the doctrine category). Such changes can result in differences that become a source of contention and eventually result in a church split. In recent times, views on abortion and same gender relationships have risen toward the status of doctrine and are causing much disruption within denominations. There also seems to be a growing trend for denominational churches to have a kinship with political agendas, which generates strong personal opinions that can be divisive. But as we can learn from Wesley and Whitefield, relations can remain amicable and Christian unity can be maintained between those of differing theological understandings.

Whitefield and Wesley remained friends through it all, with Whitefield requesting Wesley to present the sermon at his memorial service. In Wesley's memorial to Whitefield he recognized their disagreement, but also their unity as they *agreed to disagree*. Here is an excerpt from that sermon.

> And, first, let us keep close to the grand scriptural doctrines which he [George Whitefield] everywhere delivered. There are many doctrines of a less essential nature, with regard to which even the sincere children of God (such is the present weakness of human understanding) are and have been divided for many ages. In these we may think and let think; we may "agree to disagree." But, meantime, let us hold fast the essentials of "the faith which was once delivered to the saints;" and which this champion of God so strongly insisted on, at all times, and in all places![11]

---

10. Outler, *John Wesley*, 350.

11. Wesley, *The Complete Sermons*, sermon 53, 291.

Their *agree to disagree* attitude was not a casual discounting of the matter which closes off discussion. They vigorously debated each other, for they were colleagues who humbly remained open in order to fully understand the other's position.

It is also recognized that "Wesley followed a time-tested approach: 'In essentials, unity; in non-essentials, liberty; and in all things, charity.'"[12] The only problem with this seemingly good piece of advice is that there must first be agreement on what is essential and what is non-essential. What one person puts in the doctrine category, such as Whitefield's predestination, another may consider opinion. So again, relying on a commitment to agree to disagree is helpful.

We must keep the distinction between unity and uniformity in mind as we select, participate in, and support our faith communities. Humanity may love uniformity, but God loves unity. A congregation's need for uniformity can all too easily lead to splintering. At the peril of unity, a church may reason that they need everyone to interpret a particular scripture uniformly. There are many examples that show humanity's affinity for uniformity. Think about all the pending lawsuits striving to enforce uniformities mandated by homeowners' associations. If we look down on earth from a satellite, human activity is documented by looking for uniformity such as the straight lines of highways, grids of city streets, and outlines of agricultural fields. But looking down on those areas of God's creation which remain untouched by humanity, we see landscapes that have yet to be subjected to our need for uniformity. There are very few straight lines, squares, or perfect circles found among the mountains, plains, and rivers. To maintain unity, we must sometimes let go of our need for uniformity and *agree to disagree*.

Twenty-first Century

In the last decades there has been a shift in how people select a faith community. Less significance is given to denominational affinity. This trend is demonstrated by the number of churches that have been renamed in order to drop the reference to their denominational roots. A denominational label infers institutionalization which has a negative connotation in today's society. But the affiliation of a group of churches has a positive side, and many churches that start out on their own eventually coalesce into a denomination. The need for standard teaching materials, the advantage of being able to serve more people by pooling resources, and the economic advantages of sharing facilities all contribute to the endurance of denominations.

12. Olson et al., *Book of Discipline*, 51.

However, the tendency for human nature to value individualism is alive and well in America, with the result that people self-select into congregations that are compatible and closely aligned with their personal ideologies and values, rather than people demonstrating allegiance to any denomination. Fewer persons can even articulate the unique beliefs or practices of the denomination to which they belong. This is not all bad, for it has strengthened the growing ecumenical movement that seeks to find the common ground of faith and advance unity among denominations, churches, and all Christian assemblies. In speaking of ecumenical efforts, theologian Veli-Matti Kärkkäinen stated:

> To rightly understand this goal of ecumenism, one must keep in mind the fact that this concept seeks to preserve the distinction between God-given unity as gift and the human response to God's action and desire. Consequently, it is not the task of the ecumenical movement—or any other human organization for that matter—to create unity between the churches, but rather to give form to the unity already created by God. In other words, since God has created one church of Christ on earth, let Christians then live up to that fact in empirical life.[13]

We need be aware of some of the subtle ways we might be contributing to disunity in order to avoid them. There are many forms of unethical behavior by churches today that retard ecumenism, or the unity among churches. Kärkkäinen lists some of these unethical activities that were identified during the Roman Catholic-Pentecostal International Dialogue:

- All ways of promoting our own community of faith that are intellectually dishonest, such as contrasting an ideal presentation of our own community with the weaknesses of another Christian community

- All intellectual laziness and culpable ignorance that neglect readily accessible knowledge of the other's tradition

- Every willful misinterpretation of the beliefs and practices of other Christian communities[14]

We need not let our narrow theological constructs, incomplete understandings of God and scripture, organizational differences, or insistence on uniformity threaten our spiritual unity. There is much biblical evidence for respecting diversity within the contexts in which we live. However, what we hold in common, the Spirit of Christ living within us, provides strength for

---

13. Kärkkäinen, *Introduction to Ecclesiology*, 85.

14. Kärkkäinen, *Introduction to Ecclesiology*, 90.

maintaining our unity among this diversity. If we make anything else the uniting force such as the organizational structure of the church, denominational allegiance, approaches to the administration of the sacraments, liturgies, leadership patterns, a strong pastoral leader, a building, the style of worship, or the music, then the unity will eventually dissolve. As we humbly engage with God and listen for the Holy Spirit in our search for universal truths in order to live faithful lives, we can transcend divisions and distractions as we "make every effort to maintain the unity of the Spirit in the bond of peace" (Eph 4:3). And we can then join with the psalmist in expressing "how very good and pleasant it is when kindred live together in unity" (Ps 133:1).

5

Salvation: Can It Be Defined?

FEW SUBJECTS GARNER MORE questions than salvation. In a Christian context, when we hear the question *Have you been saved?* what comes to mind? Usually the original question spawns more questions. What are we saved from? How are we saved? Why are we saved? Is everyone saved? How does being saved impact daily life? Many only think of salvation in terms of going to heaven when they die. While salvation does encompass the future, it is thoroughly relevant to the present and also embraces the past. One of the difficulties with succinctly defining salvation is that it cannot be explained without reference to other Christian concepts and doctrines. An understanding of salvation requires consideration of Jesus Christ's life, death, and resurrection, as well as the concepts of atonement, justification, and sanctification. Although the terminology traditionally used to discuss salvation is uniquely the language of the church and not common to every-day conversations, this need not be a reason to shy away from discussion, for salvation is very much a part of our everyday lives.

Another reason there are few in-depth discussions is that there are diverse theories of salvation currently adhered to by various Christian groups. Regardless of these differences, there is general agreement that salvation, in its most basic sense, is the activity of God through Jesus Christ and the Holy Spirit to bring about healing of all creation. The differing understandings stretch back to the beginning of the church and contribute to the distinction between Catholic and Protestant theology. However, when examined in total, these theological variances form a complete and rich understanding of salvation. These variants are the result of different interpretations of the extensive demonstrations of salvation dispersed throughout the Old and New Testaments. The biblical manifestations of salvation take place within many historical eras, as well as a variety of cultural and social settings, and concern both believers and unbelievers. A clear and concise synthesis of salvation is a challenge no matter how many words are used, doctrines espoused, or theories constructed. Any definition will inevitably be incomplete, for God's work to restore creation to its intended glory goes deeper than words can communicate.

Biblical History

Salvation addresses humanity's broken relationships and how they are healed. Trouble began early. Adam and Eve demonstrated a broken relationship with God in the garden of Eden as they ate the forbidden fruit. They also experienced a damaged relationship with each other as Adam pointed blame toward Eve, while Eve countered that claim by blaming the serpent (Gen 3). Trouble continued as their first son, Cain, succumbed to jealousy and killed their second son, Abel (Gen 4). The inability to live in a way that is in our best interest and in the best interest of those we share the world with is why we are in need of salvation. It is a problem as old as time. We fail to live according to God's will.

The Old Testament reveals that God immediately took the initiative by embarking on a path toward restoration and healing through covenants with humanity. God's early covenant (Gen 9:1–17), which was spoken to Noah, was *universal* in nature. This covenant was between God and *all* of humankind. It established a mutual relationship of abidance and blessing. In addition, this covenant remains in effect because its duration is *everlasting* (Gen 9:16) and assures us that it is always God's desire to be in a loving relationship with *all* people.

A subsequent covenant was with the select group of Abraham and his descendants (Gen 15:1–21, 17:1–27). However, this later covenant did not replace the universal and everlasting covenant that had already been established. Even though it was with a selected group of people, it was universal. Abraham's ancestral line was promised that "in you all the families of the earth shall be blessed" (Gen 12:3b). Note that the promise is to *all* families. Abraham and his descendants were the people God chose to have a decisive role in revealing God and God's will to the world. These people whom God chose would appear different because they would be governed by the laws of God. Their uniqueness would attract the attention of the wider world, bringing God's laws to light.

As we continue in the Old Testament, we find the beginnings of the fulfillment of God's promise to Abraham. Jacob, the second-generation descendent of Abraham, was given the name *Israel* (Gen 32:28, 35:10). His new name, Israel, means he has striven with God—he could discern God's voice. Jacob's sons began the lineage of the twelve tribes of Israel (Gen 49:28). This people, called Israel, were the beginning of what will be known as the Jewish people. They were the people to whom God continued to reveal himself and his purposes.

As God revealed himself to Israel, the people realized the discrepancies between their way of life and God's will for them. They could now see the results of their failing to keep God's laws and the suffering this failure caused. The sinful nature of humanity alienates people from God and from each other. God's action to heal this estrangement and deliver the people from the effects of sin is referred to as *atonement*. The Israelites' early efforts of atonement were a ritual in which the priests symbolically placed the sins of the people on the head of a goat and sent it into the wilderness (Lev 16:6–10). This annual Day of Atonement was a solemn ritual, but not without hope. The ritual, although performed by the priests, gave the people a brief glimpse of hope that their guilt, suffering, and brokenness that resulted from their sins could be removed.

Throughout the Old Testament, we continually read of the Israelites, the ones who had been chosen to serve God's purposes, falling short of God's will. God sent numerous prophets to warn the Israelites of their failings and instruct them to turn around. But still, there was no Israelite living a life of true obedience or in complete communion with God. Regardless, the Israelites continued to have hope that one day a savior would emerge. Within the historical development of the Israelites, we learn from the genealogies in scripture (Matt 1:1–16) that Jesus was born into this ancestral line of Israelites. Jesus' flesh was of the Israelites, the Jewish people, the ones to whom God had chosen to reveal himself. We also learn of Jesus' divine nature from John 1:1–18. Jesus, this unblemished human, who was also divine, would be the savior the Israelites had long expected.

Establishing language that is able to describe the fully divine and fully human nature of Jesus has been a great challenge for theologians. The linguistic struggle resulted in the christological controversies of the early centuries, and later of the Reformation. The primary issue was finding the language that could describe the two natures of Jesus without introducing heresies. The language needed to maintain monotheism (there is only one God), not introduce subordination of Jesus to God (the Son and Father are one), and not lose Jesus' simultaneous full humanity or full deity. The term *homoousios* was finally settled on to describe the relationship between Jesus and God so as to indicate they are of the same essence.

Jesus' divine nature guaranteed his true and pure obedience and communion with God. Jesus would be that Israelite who could repair and restore relationships broken by humanity's sinfulness—he would bring salvation. Jesus could now, representing all the Israelites, atone for their sins. Further, acknowledging the universal covenant, he could atone for the sins of all people. The divine Jesus, in his resurrected life, is able to bring transformation to sinful lives in order to restore their communion with God. Jesus is the blessing and salvation that was promised.

Those who recognize the work of God's salvation in Jesus are heirs of God's promise to Abraham. As Paul informs us:

> There is no longer Jew or Greek, there is no longer slave or free, there is no longer male and female; for all of you are one in Christ Jesus. (Gal 3:28)

Paul was establishing the obsolescence of any ethnic distinction among the people of God. He is saying that further fulfillment of the divine plan in the Old Testament has taken place. When God became flesh and came down to dwell among us in Jesus, and Jesus reached back up to God in his resurrection, salvation was made possible. Presently, the activity of the Holy Spirit among humanity propels each person, through God's grace, into this salvation which was made possible by Jesus Christ.

Theological History

We have reviewed from biblical accounts what God has done through history to bring about salvation. We find assurance that Jesus Christ's life, death, and resurrection have attended to the sinful nature of humanity and provide forgiveness and the fresh beginning that we, individually and universally, require. This loving action of God is so unlike any other life experience that we are left astonished upon realization of its truth. In spite of being astounded and amazed, we are also left with questions. Although these questions are secondary to the universal work of God's actions of love, we still want to grasp just how all this was accomplished. The Bible does not give us a clear explanation. As a result, over the centuries numerous atonement theories have developed. These are models for understanding the acts of God through Jesus Christ which resulted in our restoration. It is within our human nature to want to understand in some measure that which we believe by faith. This search for insight is what prompts theologians (which is all of us) to continue to examine revealed truths.

Anselm (1033–1109), archbishop of Canterbury, desired to better understand what he knew by faith. We can see this in the following excerpt from his writings.

> I do not attempt, Lord, to penetrate Thy depth, for by no means do I compare my intellect with it; but I desire to understand, to a degree, Thy truth, which my heart believes and loves. For I do not seek to understand in order that I may believe, but I believe in order that I may understand.[1]

In Anselm's pursuit of answers to his questions, his desire is not much different than any of ours. His questions outline what originators of atonement theories have been looking for throughout time. Anselm asked of himself:

> On what basis or for which urgent reasons did God become man so that by His death, as we believe and confess, He thereby gave life to the world? Why did He do this, inasmuch as it could have been done either through some other person, angel or man, or simply by His will?[2]

Many have attempted to answer these questions. There are four theories which have persisted throughout the centuries and have acquired names that are somewhat descriptive: *satisfaction, ransom, penal substitution,* and *moral influence.* Having received significant attention and longevity, these theories warrant further elaboration. But as we study these models, keep in mind that the writers of the New Testament were more concerned with the fact that the work of Jesus led to healing the relationship between God and humanity, which makes salvation possible, and less concerned about how it happens. We might also note that the theologians of the early church, who produced the great creeds which are repeated in a majority of worship services and which represent classical orthodoxy, never settled on a single model of atonement. The workings of the atonement are represented in the New Testament with such varying images that no one view is complete. One's gravitation toward a particular model is influenced in a great part by one's understanding of the relationship between God and humanity combined with the individual's life experiences.

---

1. Anslem's *Proslogion,* ch. 1, in Hägglund, *History of Theology,* 169.
2. Anselm's *Cur Deus homo,* I ch. 1, in Hägglund, *History of Theology,* 171.

Satisfaction Theory

Anselm's answer to his own questions developed into what has been termed the satisfaction theory of atonement. Anselm saw a world in which humanity was to be obedient to God's will out of respect and mutual love.[3] In view of this understanding, he saw our sinful nature as a dishonor to God. When humanity failed to honor God by not keeping God's commands, this was a grave insult to God. Anselm thought that to correct this failure of humanity, God's honor must be restored to God's satisfaction. Since it was humanity that had dishonored God, it was only a human that could give God the satisfaction necessary to restore the relationship. However, the disobedience was so grave that humanity would not be able to accomplish this restoration; it could be achieved only through the power of God. Therefore, only Jesus, who was both human and divine, could make amends for humanity's sinfulness and repair the relationship between God and humanity. Thus, Jesus' life, death, and resurrection opened the door for our salvation by satisfying the debt generated by our sins. This model therefore focuses on what God demands in order to heal and restore his honor.

Ransom Theory

Long before Anselm's satisfaction theory, the ransom theory dominated the church's view. The idea of Christ as a ransom is sometimes attributed to the theologian and early bishop of the church, Irenaeus (c. 130–200). Yet Irenaeus did not write his commentary as a theory or model of atonement, but simply as a reflection on Jesus' life, death, and resurrection. The ransom theory that ensued maintains that sinful humanity belonged to and was in bondage to Satan. Then Christ, during his death and resurrection, fought and triumphed over Satan, releasing sinners from Satan's hold. In this struggle, Christ was the ransom paid in exchange for the liberation of humanity from Satan. The similar *Christus victor* model also describes Christ as victorious over the evil powers of the world, including Satan, during his work on the cross and resurrection. Christ, through victory or purchase, freed humanity to be rejoined in a right relationship with God and each other. The focus for this model is evil's grip on humanity that results from their sinfulness. Its origins can be seen in the following scriptures.

> Since, therefore, the children share flesh and blood, he himself
> likewise shared the same things, so that through death he might

3. Hägglund, *History of Theology*, 172.

destroy the one who has the power of death, that is, the devil (Heb 2:14–15)

Everyone who commits sin is a child of the devil; for the devil has been sinning from the beginning. The Son of God was revealed for this purpose, to destroy the works of the devil. (1 John 3:8)

Penal Substitution Theory

The penal substitution theory was developed in the 1500s during the Reformation and continues to have an extensive following among some Protestant congregations today. This model discerns that sin breaks God's law and the penalty for this sinfulness is death. God is seen as a righteous judge and cannot let the breaking of his law go unpunished. Therefore, Jesus' death was substituted for the penalty of death that human sinners were to suffer. This model is similar to the satisfaction theory in that it is an appeasement of God. But instead of appeasement by satisfying God's honor, Christ suffered the death penalty to appease the breaking of God's law. We see support of this model in the following verses.

My little children, I am writing these things to you so that you may not sin. But if anyone does sin, we have an advocate with the Father, Jesus Christ the righteous; and he is the atoning sacrifice for our sins, and not for ours only but also for the sins of the whole world. (1 John 2:1–2)

Moral Influence Theory

The moral influence theory of atonement was put forth by Peter Abelard (1079–1142) shortly after Anselm proposed the satisfaction model. Abelard, like Anselm, did not support the ransom theory's assertion that Satan had a claim over humanity. In their view this idea portrayed evil as having power that rivaled God's supremacy. Additionally, Abelard did not agree with the aspect of Anselm's model which portrayed God as needing to have his honor satisfied. Abelard saw God not as requiring compensation for humanity's sinfulness, but as loving humanity so much he was willing to forgive and refresh the human heart. The following verse speaks to this love.

But God proves his love for us in that while we still were sinners Christ died for us. (Rom 5:8)

The cross Jesus bore displayed just how far God would go to love and beckon humanity's return. The world estranged itself from God, yet God made the move to love in such a great display, through the life, death, and resurrection of Jesus Christ, that humanity would be moved to repent and return to loving God and neighbor. This moral influence model of atonement advocates that as we recognize the depth of God's love through Jesus Christ we will be moved toward repentance, resulting in forgiveness and restoration of humanity's relationship to God and the world.

Application of Theology

We have seen that there are a variety of ways to express how atonement is accomplished. Some of the theories are based on imagery resembling a law court, while others are based on imagery related to grace and love. However, the models must each be considered within the cultural and social norms of the times in which they were developed. We need not press one model too far or feel a need to choose one over another. Each model, with support from scripture, uses imagery that can be of value at different times and in different situations.

When human sin is being addressed, there is a natural tendency to describe atonement in terms of a sacrifice being made to justly compensate for those sins. If humanity is envisioned as being under hostile evil powers, then the expected imagery might be of a battle and subsequent victory. If humanity is without knowledge of God's gracious nature, then images of the disclosure of God's love on the cross would be expected. In general, atonement theories begin and end with a recognition and trust that the acts of God in Jesus Christ were an expression of God's universal love. The result of this love is the promise of deliverance from evil, forgiveness of our sins, and a new fresh orientation to life. All of humanity is offered a healed and renewed relationship with God and with each other. We may never fully comprehend how the saving work of the atonement was accomplished, but how one responds to this act of God's grace is *salvation* in action.

Living Salvation

Past

God's past acts of love through the work of Christ have provided the foundation for our salvation. The understanding of salvation over the centuries has produced variances that have resulted in Christianity being partitioned into Catholics and Protestants (who themselves are divided into numerous denominations). But one point of agreement among all Christians is the understanding that salvation was made possible by God's love for humanity and is offered to humanity by Christ's atoning work and the ensuing arrival of the Holy Spirit. There may be differences of opinion in how atonement is accomplished, but there is agreement that in this divine act, a fresh start and release from all kinds of bondage awaits humanity's response.

Present

In the present, God reaches out to humanity through the Holy Spirit, bringing Christ's presence into hearts. This initiative on God's part is often referred to as *prevenient grace*—prevenient in the sense that God has taken the initiative to introduce his love to us through the Holy Spirit and God now awaits our response. A Christian's positive response to Christ's atoning work is to believe, that is, to have faith in these acts of God's love.

God's acceptance of us, even while we are sinners, and our positive response of faith in this gracious act of God is called justification. This achievement is not through our own doing but is the gift of God.

> For by grace you have been saved through faith, and this is not your own doing; it is the gift of God—not the result of works, so that no one may boast. (Eph 2:8–9)

Even though we are sinners, we have been pardoned, justified, and relieved of the burden of our sins. This divine feat may be experienced as a sudden moment of assurance, or it may be more of a gradual sense of knowing through small steps. But it is always accompanied by a desire to participate more fully in God's will for our lives and the world. For Protestants, faith is all that is required to be brought into this new relationship with God. Catholic doctrine places further obligations on persons in order to receive the gift of God's grace, including sacraments of the church.

In this new justified orientation of the Christian's life, one has faith in God's mercy and the opportunity for forgiveness and a fresh beginning. With help from the Holy Spirit, which dwells in the justified Christian, we are led to experience a contrite heart and repent of our sins. Although joined with Christ at justification, there is a continual need to transform relationships because, paradoxically, the justified are still sinners. This lifetime of growth toward conforming to God's intended goal is called *sanctification*. Participation in continued sanctification brings one individually, and the world collectively, closer to enjoying the fullness of life.

An aspect of sanctification that is crucial to enjoying the fullness of life is forgiveness and the resultant reconciliation. As Lewis Smedes stated:

> God invented forgiving as a remedy for a past that not even he could change . . . His [God's] way of forgiving is the model for our forgiving.[4]

We read about God's way of forgiving throughout the Bible.

> Put away from you all bitterness and wrath and anger and wrangling and slander, together with all malice, and be kind to one another, tenderhearted, forgiving one another, as God in Christ has forgiven you. (Eph 4:31–32)

Another model of forgiveness that describes God's way is found in Luke 15:11–32. This is the story of the prodigal son who was forgiven and welcomed back into the family. Commentaries on this story abound, in part because forgiveness is crucial for the restoration of relationships, but also because, in practice, forgiveness invokes many human emotions and thus can be complex and challenging. The appendix suggests books that can be useful in the practice of forgiveness—both in forgiving yourself and forgiving others.

We have concentrated on being saved from our sins, which is a resolute cycle of repentance, forgiveness, and healing. But God's saving grace is not limited to addressing only our sinful nature. We are also in need of saving grace that addresses deeper feelings of remorse, grief, and despair and many more situations of suffering that need healing. Scars remain from the wounds of all varieties of suffering. To soothe these, God's grace offers peace to the soul. Such peace comes through the Holy Spirit and is described in Philippians 4:7 as "the peace of God, which surpasses all understanding." While our sins are blotted out through prayerful repentance, a prayerful relationship with God also brings peace to other situations that require healing.

Christ's saving work also has a wider, more universal bearing on humanity in the present that should not be overlooked. This is the expansion of the kingdom of God. Jesus spoke frequently of the kingdom of God. While it is difficult to define, a good summation is put forth with these words: "The kingdom of God is . . . the time and place where God's power and will hold sway."[5] The kingdom of God was inaugurated with Jesus' life on earth and was further brought to earth after his resurrection with the outpouring of

---

4. Smedes, *The Art of Forgiving*, 117.
5. Stanton, *The Gospels and Jesus*, 195–96.

the Holy Spirit on humanity. Now Christians, restored, healed, and filled with the power of the Holy Spirit, can further the kingdom of God on earth through acts of discipleship. Jesus' teachings while on earth demonstrated the acts of discipleship which bring the kingdom of God to earth. From Jesus' teachings we learn how to live by his example, which creates a sphere of the kingdom of God in the present. Through salvation, Christians are more fully equipped for discipleship, and they respond out of love because God first loved them (1 John 4:19).

Future

We have looked at salvation in terms of the past atoning work of Jesus Christ. We have looked at salvation in relation to the moment a decision to believe in Jesus Christ and his redeeming work justifies the individual and cancels their sins. And we have looked at salvation in terms of the present ongoing process of sanctification and what it means for the world. These positive changes in the life of a Christian are the result of the indwelling of the Holy Spirit, which leads to both contrite and benevolent hearts.

But what of the future? This question shifts our focus to the Christian belief that life is eternal—that we continue to live after bodily death. Many people only think of salvation in terms of this future afterlife experience. However, to think of salvation primarily in terms of being saved in order to go to heaven after death diminishes and distorts the full range of Christ's work. Salvation has an impact on eternal life, but eternal life encompasses all of life, beginning with our birth and never ending. So, if you think of salvation as determining whether you reside in heaven or hell, then heaven and hell must be considered on both sides of bodily death. While being concerned about divine judgement, we also acknowledge there is, above all, mercy in judgement. The purpose of God's just and loving judgment, which we experience through the Holy Spirit, is to lead to repentance and make room for his mercy.

We can struggle on this side, before death, alienated from God with the resultant loneliness, restlessness, and turmoil, or we can live on this side with the heavenly peace of salvation. The gospel message on this side of eternity is one of calling us to forgiveness, reconciliation, and healing of our relationships. There is no reason to think that God's benevolent character is any different on the other side of eternity. We do not know what awaits us after death; it is beyond our witnessing. What we do know is that God *desires* salvation for *everyone*.

Also, what we do know is that the goal of salvation is for God's kingdom to reign throughout creation and that this reign will happen in the sphere of the saving work of Jesus Christ. Although God's saving grace benefits the individual, it will in turn benefit the world. Saved individuals have the joy and the responsibility to participate in extending the kingdom of God on earth. The saved individual's life, when being lived out of transformation by the Holy Spirit, reflects what God desires for the whole world. Changes in the world which reflect more and more of God's love and come closer and closer to manifesting the kingdom of God depend on saved individuals' inner realignment of heart and resultant acts of discipleship. *Thy kingdom come, they will be done, on earth as it is in heaven.*

6

Church: What Function Does It Serve?

THE CHURCH—WHAT IS IT? What is its purpose? Does the church advance the kingdom of God on earth? Do people find joy, strength, and hope in the church? Does the church burden itself with trying to be too many things to too many people? Does it spend too much time and money to sustain the institution? Given the news headlines of failings and divisiveness in the churches, has the church lost its way? There appear to be many reasons that could lead us to dismiss and abandon the church. But before we surrender to that impulse, let us take an objective look at the church and its purpose. We can begin by asking, did Jesus even intend to establish the church? This last question might not be asked by many in the congregations, but the answer takes us to the dawn of the church and provides the background necessary to consider the purposes of the church.

Jesus and the Birth of the Church

Jesus antedates the church. While it is therefore possible to examine and reflect on Jesus' intentions prior to the existence of the church, it is inconceivable to consider the church without Jesus. We consider Jesus' role in the foundation of the church because it will enlighten our assessment of today's church. We have been exposed to the rich traditions and history of the church, and these have certainly influenced us, leading to suppositions about the church and Jesus' role in establishing it. However, as we begin our exploration, it will be helpful to set aside any assumptions imposed by our heritage and church traditions and look to Jesus alone. We cannot assume that just because the church emerged, this outcome was Jesus' intention. Our source will be the New Testament, specifically the Gospels. Although the Gospels were written years after Jesus' earthly ministry, they provide testimony to Jesus' role in the emergence of the church. The aims of Jesus that can be detected from these writings include fulfilling God's promise of restoring Israel, bringing the kingdom of God to earth, and providing the path to salvation. Although these purposes are inextricably linked, we will look at them separately.

Jesus entered a world of the temple and synagogues. He valued the temple's sanctity and referred to it as his Father's house (Luke 2:49) and a house of prayer (Matt 21:13). It was the *church* of the day and was populated by the Jewish community—the people of God, Israel. Jesus made use of the synagogues throughout Galilee, teaching and proclaiming the good news of the kingdom (Matt 4:23) and reinterpreting Israel's laws in the light of his message of love (Matt 22:34–40). He was neither asking or expecting the people to abandon Judaism, nor was he founding a separate or new institution; he was restoring the existing one. Theologians B. Meyer, E. P. Sanders, and N. T. Wright all regard the calling of the twelve disciples to be symbolic of calling the twelve tribes of Israel and consider this act as evidence that one of Jesus' aims was the restoration of Israel.[1]

Jesus came first to the temple people. His disciples were sent on their way with the instructions: "Go nowhere among the Gentiles, and enter no town of the Samaritans, but go rather to the lost sheep of the house of Israel" (Matt 10:5b–6). Jesus invited the people of God, who had returned from physical exile, to now complete their return from exile by receiving the new life he offered them. Jesus was pointing Israel to the way of true freedom from exile and into a new relationship with God that included restoration and redemption. Arthur Patzia so succinctly states, "Jesus sought to establish the *true* Israel, not a *new* Israel."[2] Israel was to be transformed into what it was truly intended to be. This true Israel would proclaim Jesus as the Messiah and follow Jesus' instructions on fulfilling the law with love and mercy (Matt 12:1–8). Jesus exclaimed, "I tell you something greater than the temple is here" (Matt 12:6).

Consistent with God's early covenants, Jesus expanded his mission beyond the people of Israel to all humanity. There are early examples that even before this expansion his message did not completely ignore the non-Jewish population. For instance, he did not exclusively teach in the synagogues but also preached in public settings. Continuing to expand his ministry to the

1. Wright, *Jesus and the Victory*, 104.
2. Patzia, *Emergence of the Church*, 60.

world, he healed a Canaanite's daughter (Matt 15:21–28), and the servant of a non-Jewish military officer (Matt 8:5–13). That Jesus' mission expanded to the entire world is most clearly seen in Matthew 28:18–20 as he sends his disciples to spread the gospel message to *all nations*.

As the disciples went into the world, they were to proclaim the good news that the kingdom of heaven has come near (Matt 10:7). That is, Jesus has brought God's power, will, and authority to earth. The large number of Jesus' teachings concerning the kingdom of God in the Gospels leaves little doubt that Jesus came to bring the kingdom of God to earth and wanted his followers to understand what this meant.[3] There are numerous parables that begin with the words "the kingdom of God is like." In fact, the phrase "the kingdom of God" or "kingdom of heaven" can be found 162 times in the New Testament.[4] While we experience the hope that the kingdom of God will be more fully realized in the future (Matt 6:10), there are already glimpses of it on earth (Luke 17:21).

You might be wondering at this point how Jesus' goals of restoring the true Israel and bringing God's kingdom to earth relate to the founding of the church. Jesus message to Israel was not welcomed by everyone. Some of the people of the synagogues not only rejected Jesus as the Messiah, but felt his teachings were blasphemy. Others feared Jesus posed a challenge to their authority. The kingdom of God that Jesus brought did not look like what the leaders of the Jewish faith expected. Allegiance to Jesus' message would eventually place his followers outside the synagogue, and as they grew in number, they began to crystalize into their own community. The end result was the creation of *two* separate communities among God's people. But it would be an oversimplification to say that because of this split Jesus intentionally founded the church. Jesus' coming to earth was the force that polarized the religious community into two groups, but the most we can say is that while this circumstance did in fact result in the foundation of the church, Jesus' role in this outcome was primarily a passive one.

Up to this point we have looked at the role of Jesus' earthly life. However, the days from Jesus' death and resurrection to the sending of the Holy Spirit—the days between Good Friday and Pentecost (which coincided with the days between Passover and the Jewish agricultural festival of Pentecost) contained the momentous events that solidified the church. The discovery of the empty tomb, the appearances of Jesus to his followers after his death, and the observance of his ascension served to give his followers confidence

---

3. Wright, *Jesus and the Victory*, 663–70. This appendix contains a well-organized list of kingdom of God passages.

4. Balz and Schneider, *Exegetical Dictionary*, 1:201.

in his identity as Lord and Messiah. These events further elucidated Jesus' mission to his disciples and what this meant for humanity. In Acts 1:6–11, before Jesus' ascension, he tells the apostles that "you will be my witnesses in Jerusalem, in all Judea and Samaria, and to the ends of the earth." Then they waited in Jerusalem for the promised Holy Spirit. Raymond Brown observed that these and other instructions that Jesus left with the apostles "makes the church both explicable and essential."[5] It was not the church that Jesus brought them together to form, but they were brought together for a common purpose, resulting in the formation of the fellowship that would become the church.

The culminating event was the receiving of the Holy Spirit as described in Acts 2. The sounds and sights amazed the crowd, which included people from diverse regions who had come to celebrate the Jewish festival. This event filled Jesus' followers with confidence and power to preach the gospel message of repentance and restoration. The disciples (learners) now became the apostles (teachers). This community of believers, filled with the enabling Holy Spirit, could now pass on the message of God's redeeming gift to humanity. This gift of the Spirit further polarized Jesus' followers from the non-believing Jews. The creation of a second and separate religious community was inevitable, as the band of believers, now without their visible leader, but with a deeper understanding of their mission, solidified into an even tighter and more established community. The Greek word used in the scriptures which translates into English as *community* came into widespread use just after the resurrection.[6] It was the saving work of Christ that began to solidify the Christian community or church. But again, the aim does not appear to be the foundation of a church, but rather the fulfillment of a promise accomplished by the offer of salvation through the work of Christ. Salvation is not obtained by joining a religious institution but by coming to have faith in the work of Jesus.

In summary Jesus, the Messiah, the Son of God, came to restore Israel, announce the arrival of the kingdom of God, and bring salvation. He clashed with the agendas of many of the religiously and politically powerful. He called followers, healed, taught, demonstrated a new order of justice, and interjected the love of God and neighbor into the interpretation of the law. But there is simply not enough evidence to say that Jesus intended to establish the church or any religious community distinct from Judaism, but rather that he sought to transform Judaism. Even though the aims of Jesus lay outside of the establishment of the church, the church did originate from

5. Brown, *Churches the Apostles Left*, 63.

6. Cwiekowski, *Beginnings of the Church*, 60.

the impacts of Jesus' ministry. Christianity formed alongside Judaism and the church alongside the synagogue. And it would be the church that provided a framework for the continuation of Jesus' work.

The Church Comes in View

The most basic definition of the church is a community of people who, bound together by the Holy Spirit, share in witnessing to Jesus Christ. The church, beginning as a disordered group of followers of Christ, bore the responsibility of passing the gospel message forward. We can find the purpose of the church in the activities of the apostles as they responded to the instructions Jesus left them. Jesus expected the community of believers to go and make disciples (Matt 28:19), feed his sheep (John 21:17), and worship in spirit and truth (John 4:24). These acts of teaching, serving, and worshiping were to be carried out in the unity of love (John 13:34–35) and while living a consecrated life (Rom 12:1–8). Those who endeavored to live this life were the church. The church was not an institution, but a group of people.

After Jesus' resurrection, the apostles found themselves with increasing concerns for ensuring the transmission of Christ's message of salvation and love to the next generation. They began to preserve the message by writing it down and distributing these documents to gatherings of believers. They warded off misrepresentations of the message and made decisions concerning new situations that had not been specifically addressed by Jesus' discourses. Their clarifications were only the beginning, for even today we continue to interpret and teach fresh ideas as new situations arise. Theologian E. Schweizer saw this need for continual interpretation as "what lays the foundation of the church."[7] These matters propelled the apostles, as well as later believers, toward more organization. And thus began the gradual climb into the institutional church of today.

Assessing Contemporary Churches

Although the churches of today sit within a different culture than experienced by the apostles, their role remains the same. The church endures as a group of believers whose obligation is to worship, teach, and serve in a way that glorifies God. The role of today's church is therefore the same as the one left by Jesus to his disciples. It has been cultivated for centuries. However,

---

7. Schweizer, *Church Order*, 59.

even with this extensive history on which to draw, putting the instructions of Jesus into practice for each new generation and cultural situation can be daunting and can imperil the church's foremost roles. It is appropriate to occasionally review these roles as we assess the church.

The Church Worships

Although a Christian can worship independently, the church's worship services provision the mandate to worship God. Chapter 7 further explores worship but does not address the sacraments practiced in these services. This dimension of the church is worthy of exploration, for these sacred acts nurture the relationship between the people and God, as well as cultivate community among the people as they profess the faith they hold in common. Christ taught the practice of two sacraments, namely baptism and the Lord's Supper. The liturgy used in these sacraments recites the entire gospel message of restoration and communion with God, thus participation in them bears witness to the grace of God. Along with the outward ritual is an inward reality that strengthens the individual's faith and proceeds to collectively build up the faith of the community. As people participate in these acts of commitment, God's grace is imparted, affirming and nourishing their faith. Through these rituals the participants experience the Holy Spirit leading them into deeper union with Christ. The merit to the individual is likewise experienced by the whole church community as these sacraments underscore the unity they share in Christ.

It is unfortunate that there has not been full agreement among churches with regard to the understanding and administration of the sacraments. However, we find hope in the fact that Christian churches the world over practice these two sacraments.[8] Overshadowing the variances in the church's sacramental practices is the universal understanding that Christ ordained them, they contribute to the unity of the faithful, and God's grace is present in them.

The Church Teaches

Everyone who attends church does not have the same knowledge or maturity of the faith. This disparity makes the teaching role of the church critical and drives the church to be a community that encourages each other. This

8. Scriptural references to the Lord's Supper can be found the following chapters: Matt 26, Mark 14, Luke 22, and 1 Cor 11.

encouragement takes the form of sharing and clarifying the gospel message. There are two aspects to this dissemination of the faith. One is to spread the message to unbelievers through evangelism, while the other is to bring believers to deeper knowledge of God's restorative work. Jesus seems to have had no design for transmitting his message without the assistance of his followers. It has been noted that "the church is never more than one generation away from extinction; all it would take is for a single generation not to hand the word on."[9] However, throughout two millennia, formal teaching and living examples have kept the message flourishing. It has survived by being shared among the followers of Christ, coupled with the Holy Spirit's guidance in these individual's lives. No generation has been without witnesses to Christ's work. Even when persecution has tried to bury the message, it has endured.

Paul demonstrated the continuous transmission of the gospel when he said, "For I received from the Lord what I also handed on to you" (1 Cor 11:23a). We can find numerous instructions throughout the New Testament that demonstrate Jesus' intention for his disciples to carry the message forward and continue to grow in their understanding of God's will.

> Then he [Jesus] said to them [his disciples], "These are my words that I spoke to you while I was still with you—that everything written about me in the law of Moses, the prophets, and the psalms must be fulfilled." Then he opened their minds to understand the scriptures, and he said to them, "Thus it is written, that the Messiah is to suffer and to rise from the dead on the third day, and that repentance and forgiveness of sins is to be proclaimed in his name to all nations, beginning from Jerusalem. You are witnesses of these things." (Luke 24:44–48)

Just as the previous scripture presents the opening of their minds to understanding, Romans 12:2 reminds us that we are to be continually transformed by the renewing of our minds.

> Do not be conformed to this world, but be transformed by the renewing of your minds, so that you may discern what is the will of God—what is good and acceptable and perfect.

Our minds are to be renewed as we habitually seek to know God's will. This expansion of our minds requires ongoing thought, searching, and learning. It is the role of the church to keep offering opportunities for the renewal of the mind. This renewal, aided by the Spirit, paves the way to discern the will of God. The words in Romans do not limit this understanding of God's

9. Wright, *John for Everyone*, 98–99.

will to simple legal and moral rules but encourage transformation of one's thought patterns into God's will. This process is one that Christians continue their entire lives and the church, that is, the universal group of fellow Christians which make up the church, is to take part in it by educating each other.

The faithful, gathered inside churches, have many opportunities to fulfill the vital role of teaching one another. It is crucial for Christians to accurately understand that their faith and the discipline of study is foundational to this end. Whether one approaches study through reading, prayer, sermons, church school classes, or formal advanced education, the purpose of this education is to grasp knowledge of God's will in order to live accordingly.

The Church Serves

Once the Christian church has sought to know God's will, it has a responsibility for the mission revealed to it. This leads us to the third role of the church—service to the world. The knowledge now gained from renewal of the mind directs the hands and feet in pursuit of the mission each has been called to. Executing this call is doing the work of God, which expands the kingdom of God on earth. Jesus said to his disciples, "As the Father has sent me, so I send you" (John 20:21b).

We are to care for the needs of all God's people. There is no better way to describe this role of service than to look at John 21:15–17. Jesus has just fed the disciples from a miraculously large catch of fish. He now asks Peter three times: "Do you love me?" Peter replies in the affirmative each time, to which Jesus responds, "Feed my lambs," "Tend my sheep," "Feed my sheep." These three questions to the disciple who had denied Jesus three times prompted the forgiveness that would allow Peter to get back to work. We do not need to be perfect before we are of use to God; we simply need to be upheld by God's grace. We may be distracted by the memory of past failures, like Peter's denial of Jesus, but we are still tasked with the work of shepherding those in need. The sooner we allow God to restore us from any distracting guilt of our sinful nature or to heal life's faultless hurts, the sooner and larger our contribution will be toward his earthly kingdom. Eliminating these distractions by restoring our relationship with God and with others restores our full potential and keeps us moving forward. God trusts us with his work, and there is much work to be done.

The question often arises, "Do I need to be a Christian to do God's work?" It is obvious that much good can also come from the work of those who do not profess faith in Christ. In fact, today there is a proliferation of altruistic nonprofit organizations that are very proficient at achieving good works. More and more often our culture requires specialized knowledge to accomplish goals of serving. We have become a legalistic society with complicated requirements for providing the basics of life such as food, health care, housing, transportation, and education. The local church cannot possibly be proficient in each of these. Doing good work is doing God's work no matter how it is organizationally founded and carried out. Many Christians find their work through these organizations suitable to fulfill their calling. It is people, not institutions, that serve one another. It is people who do the work of Christ inside and outside of the institutional church. God lays the obligation to serve on the heart of people and it is their responsibility to respond. The church's role is to encourage each other in doing good work and to support these endeavors with their resources.

The Church Continues

We have looked at the three tasks the church is commissioned to sustain: worship, teaching, and service. How well these three pursuits are being accomplished provides a means for assessing the state of the church. At a deeper level the health of the church is also gauged by its fidelity in recognizing the saving work of Christ. Faith in the gospel message creates an opening for the Holy Spirit to speak to the church. The role of the church is not to bring salvation to its people—that is between God and the individual. The church is to nurture the people in their faith. This nurturing not only applies to believers, but also seekers with hope they will find faith. It is only when the message of Christ is proclaimed and received that the church has a hope of fulfilling its charge. It is again important to underscore that the Christian message has not changed, even though the culture in which we proclaim Christ has changed. We do not hold to the message merely to cling to the past but because it is true authentic Christianity. "Jesus Christ is the same yesterday and today and forever" (Heb 13:8). However, to continue to pass on the Christian message, its presentation must be through contemporary modes of communication. It is through good communication that the message can take root.

The secular world, consistent with the historical pattern, presses in on the church. Churches chase the culture by trying new ways to present the message, often finding that our fast-paced society outruns them. The worldly and the godly simultaneously vie for our attention. The church must carefully discern how to keep uppermost the message that it was established to carry, even as it tries new innovations to bring that message to the ears of a new culture. As N. T. Wright said, "Novelty for the sake of novelty is just as sterile as custom for the sake of custom."[10] We would do well to keep these thoughts in mind as the business of the church is carried out in the midst of competing allegiances and obligations.

The church must be careful to stay away from the things that diminish a church. Is the church spending too much energy conforming to the world? Are its constituents or clergy clamoring for prestige or position? Is attendance simply habitual and of no spiritual consequence? Is service rendered for self-seeking praise? If such questions are being considered, it can be a warning sign that the church is drifting toward the worldly. Moreover, if members can hear the "woe to you scribes and Pharisees" phrases of Matthew 23 echoing in their head, it may be time for reassessment.

On the other side of the coin are the things that build the body of Christ. The people of the church find that their most sacred and life changing moments happen in the assemblies of the church. Celebrations of birth, marriage, death, confirmation, baptism, and the Lord's Supper are all found in the church. These occasions are the ones that make us pause and acquiesce to the grandeur of God. As these occasions are marked in the presence of the entire congregation, a strong community develops. The church is about sharing our lives with each other as the Holy Spirit draws us together in vital unity, which is a hallmark of the kingdom of God.

Someone once asked me, "What kind of church do you belong to?" That was a nebulous but very good question. Perhaps it is a question every person should ask of a church they belong to or are considering calling home. Were they asking how well does the church worship, teach, and serve? Or was the questioner simply wanting to know the denominational affiliation? Were they asking about theological doctrines or social principles? Did they want to know if it had a liberal or conservative political leaning? Did they want to know the style of the worship services? Or perhaps they just wanted to know if it served coffee and donuts? Have you ever stopped to think about what kind of church you want to belong to?

In John 17 Jesus prays as his work on earth is coming to a close. He prays for his disciples and for the future universal collection of believers. He is revealing his hopes for this community that will follow, which we know as the church. His primary aspiration is for its unity. There is an internal unity that all believers share, evidenced by the love that they have for each other. The world will know they are looking at Christ's followers by this unity and will come to believe. He also prayed that their joy would be complete.

10. Wright, *Matthew for Everyone*, 192.

By their belief, Christ would be in them and they would share in his joy. No longer able to remain with them as their protecting shepherd, he also prayed that they would continue to be protected from worldly wickedness. He prayed they would represent Christ to the world so that the world may believe. Jesus' prayer is yet to be fully realized, but it gives the church direction. Every generation of Christians are to work toward universal unity, expressed in love, and thus lead the world into God's kingdom.

Lament for the Church

If you are devoted to the institutional church and content with your assessment of it, I suggest that you read no further in this chapter. However, if you are not satisfied, then by all means read on. It is not exclusively through praise, glowing words, and positive comportment that God's work is advanced. Like Jeremiah, the crying prophet, we weep and groan for what is lost. Has the church lost its way? Do you grieve, groan, and shed tears for the current chaos in the church?

As church membership dropped in America, research identified increasing numbers of *nones*, those who claimed no interest in religion. So, the church made itself more attractive to the culture—updating the music, modernizing the language, and increasing the entertainment level. These things made the gospel message more accessible and increased the visibility of its relevance to people's lives. There were some successes. But in many cases, it only raised the entertainment level and did not result in deep, transformative Christian faith.

Another segment of the population that is now missing from the church are those who felt the institutional church "stifled" their "ability to engage with each other and their communities."[11] These Christians ultimately compartmentalized their faith from the institutional church and, although reluctantly, walked away from the church. Sociologist Josh Packard identified and popularized the name of this group as *dones*, saying these people are not *done* with their faith but are *done* with the church.[12] Alarms should have gone off with this discovery. If the church stifles people from engaging with each other and their communities, there is no possibility it can exhibit the love and unity that draws the world to Christ and brings God's kingdom to earth. These were the exact attributes that Jesus prayed for his followers to exhibit in order to continue his mission—unity and love. There is evidence which suggests the church is in trouble from more than the

11. Packard and Hope, *Church Refugees*, 7.
12. Packard and Hope, *Church Refugees*, 7.

existence of the *nones* and the *dones*. I am sure you can name shortcomings and blunders that chip away at its foundation. Topping the list would be the well-publicized moral transgressions of various church leaders. We rightfully cry out to God for guidance, authentically lamenting these failings.

Laments are not futile or pointless groaning and grieving. They are passionate songs. They are filled with love, even though they may not sound like it, because no one grieves what they do not cherish. We can trust that the Holy Spirit hears our laments, for the shouting and weeping are foremost a prayer. So, cry out to God. Fully express what is absent in the church. Fully express where the worldly has overlaid the church. And then listen. Laments begin with raised voices. As we exhaust ourselves, release control, and quietly listen, the lament, in an unforeseen way, turns into hope for the future. We hope that the church can slough off its worldly shell and emerge into a new life filled with worship, learning, and service. Jesus sent his disciples into the world reminding them (and us), "I am with you always, to the end of age" (Matt 28:20b). The church cannot expand the kingdom of God in its own strength, nor does it have to, for Christ's spirit is always present in us.

7

Worship: What Is Its Meaning and Purpose?

WORSHIP CARRIES VARIOUS MEANINGS. It can be a noun meaning the adoration which is offered to an object of worth, or it can be a verb describing the actions engaged in offering adoration to an object of worth. Consequently, to fully define any worship, a description of the adored object along with the activities which demonstrate homage to it must be elaborated. The activities that expound worship can be diverse and take on many forms. But more significant than the form of adoration is the object of worship. It must be known and considered worthy. Without believing in the worthiness of the object, why worship it? Closely tied to understanding the worthiness of the object is to be clear about the purpose of offering worship. Is the reason for engaging in worship confined to some uplifting feeling it generates, or is there a more noble driving force? We will explore Christian worship in terms of who, how, and why we worship.

The Christian's object of worship is solely God in Jesus Christ. It is important to be clear about *who* one believes Jesus Christ to be, because that will guide the *how* and *why* of one's engagement in worship. Again, to effect worship one must believe in the worth of the object—Jesus Christ. This chapter follows the chapter on salvation because it is an informed understanding of God's desire to be in relationship with us and his ability to forgive, heal, and love that brings us to know the worthiness of the one worshiped. But these restorative victories that we as individuals enjoy as we worship are only the beginning of its purpose. When we begin to fully take in the enormity of God's creation and what Christ accomplished for us, our hearts fill with adoration. It is the head and heart together that inform, inspire, and give rise to worship. As the knowledge of God infuses our thoughts, we leave our own self-interest behind and with a full heart begin to humbly worship God. In this abandonment of self-centeredness, God can reach our hearts and guide us into actions that bring his kingdom to earth. We bring a measure of God's kingdom to earth each time we allow the Holy Spirit to motivate and equip us to carry out the ethical responsibilities and deeds which honor God. These deeds can have far-reaching influence as they penetrate the world with God's love. This is the inherent purpose of authentic Christian worship.

To bring to light our understanding of the God whom Christians worship, we will look at the Old and New Testament accounts of God's actions toward humanity and the people's response to God. We will examine worship in the early church and then follow with a look into expressions of worship in today's church services. It is common today for people to think of worship in terms of a weekly worship service. I suggest that if we primarily think of worship as taking place in a gathering that fits into a slot on our calendars and attach it to a particular time and place, then we have misidentified worship and drained it of its full purpose and power, and we will be left disheartened. As we explore the scriptures, we will find worship to be more than compartmentalized segments of an individual's life. We will see worship ingrained in every realm of existence.

Worship in the Old Testament

Beginning with the Old Testament writings, we find the people deepening their worship by establishing an understanding of who God is. God's worthiness was continually brought to the fore by recollection of his creation, saving acts, and blessings of provision, as well as acknowledgment of his constant presence and protection. A number of feasts, festivals, and rituals were celebrated to honor God. These events both taught new generations about God and refreshed the memories of the longstanding worshipers. Thus, God's nature and eminence were continually before the people. Leviticus 23 describes this sacred calendar of events. These remembrances are not just for God's people of long ago; their meaning and significance continue to inform people of God's nature today.

The most familiar celebration, Passover, recalls God's deliverance of his people from Egyptian slavery (Exod 12). Closely tied to Passover is the festival of Unleavened Bread, which commemorates their hasty, but successful, flight from Egypt (Deut 16). Continuing to identify the saving acts of God, we read of the Day of Atonement, which provides a solemn ritual for giving hope to the contrite people by symbolically carrying away their sins (Lev 16). There were also festivals that proceeded through the agricultural seasons. These invoked remembrance of God's covenant with the people to bless them and their land (Lev 26:3–5). These festivals reveal thankfulness for rain and successful harvests. For example, the Festival of Weeks is at the time the wheat yields its bounty, and the Festival of Booths celebrates the harvest of grapes and olives. All the festivals, feasts, and rituals taken together reminded the people of God's covenant with them. These observances brought the worshipers into a pattern of continual recognition of the blessings they received. In these practices they learned who it was they worship.

In addition to these practices, which helped expound God's nature to the gathered community, the people were individually aware of God's presence with them. In Exodus 25:8 the Lord said to Moses, "And have them make me a sanctuary, so that I may dwell among them." This dwelling place, the tabernacle, assured the people that God was among them. However, God's presence was not limited to this structure, nor was God's presence limited to the later structures of God's dwelling, namely, the temple and the synagogue. Not everyone lived near these sites. As seen in the Psalms, one worshiped God by praying and bowing down to him wherever they were—on pilgrimages to these special dwelling places, in their homes, or as they worked in the fields. The people knew God to be in their midst and their response was thankfulness and homage. These excerpts from Psalm 96 demonstrate their awareness of the supremacy of the God of their worship:

> For great is the Lord, and greatly to be praised; he is to be revered above all gods. (Ps 96:4)

> Ascribe to the Lord the glory due his name. (Ps 96:8a)

> The Lord is King! (Ps 96:10a)

The responses to this recognition of God's worthiness were wide-ranging expressions of worship which included sacrificial offerings of grains and animals, personal expressions of silently bowing down, as well as flamboyant praises of song and dance. These excerpts from Psalm 95 demonstrate these responses to the God of their worship:

> O come, let us sing to the Lord; let us make a joyful noise to the rock of our salvation! Let us come into his presence with thanksgiving; let us make a joyful noise to him with songs of praise! (Ps 95:1–2)

> O come, let us worship and bow down, let us kneel before the
> Lord, our Maker! (Ps 95:6)

We can see a summary of the *who* and *how* of worship in Deuteronomy 10–11. This section of scripture reveals what the Lord requires. They are to worship the Lord God alone, who did great and awesome things for them. They worship not only through praise and bowing down, but in walking in all his ways, loving him, keeping his commandments, serving him with all their heart and soul, loving the strangers among them, and teaching the children the words of the Lord. Micah 6:8 is another summary of how they were to come before the Lord. They were to do justice, love kindness, and walk humbly with God. Their worship encompassed all aspects of their lives. Worship was not a solitary activity of homage but a life of reverence and obedience. And why were they to worship? For their own well-being (Deut 10:13), so that they may have strength (Deut 11:8), and that they may be blessed (Deut 11:27). Their blessing was not just for them, as we learned from Gen 12:2, for God's people are blessed to be a blessing to all people. Their blessings were to be shared among all people as a way to bind them together in God's love.

Worship in the New Testament

As we begin exploring the New Testament, we find a continuance of the Old Testament's declaration of God dwelling among the people. The priests' energies remained focused on activities at the temple or synagogue, which informed the people of who God is. The people continued to see these places as signposts or assurances that God was with them, and their knowledge of God continued to inspire worship.

The New Testament then records how God fulfilled his promise of sending a savior, the Messiah. John 1:14 tells us that God became flesh in Jesus and dwelt among them. God, no longer shielded from view, walked in the flesh among the people addressing the priests in the synagogues and the people where they lived.

> Then Jesus went about all the cities and villages, teaching in their synagogues, and proclaiming the good news of the kingdom, and curing every disease and every sickness (Matt 9:35)
>
> Now when Jesus had finished saying these things, the crowds were astounded at his teachings, for he taught them as one having authority, and not as their scribes. (Matt 7:28)

The people were being increasingly informed about who God is and what was expected of them. The befitting relationships with God and each other were expounded as Jesus carried news to them through his teachings and through the foretelling of his death and resurrection. Their worship would be further transformed by the dwelling of the Holy Spirit in their hearts. Jesus anticipated the influence of the Holy Spirit in our lives as he says to a woman at Jacob's well:

> "But the hour is coming, and is now here, when the true wor-
> shipers will worship the Father in spirit and truth, for the Father
> seeks such as these to worship him. God is spirit, and those who
> worship him must worship in spirit and truth." The woman
> said to him, "I know that the Messiah is coming" (who is called
> Christ). "When he comes, he will proclaim all things to us." Je-
> sus said to her, "I am he, the one who is speaking to you." (John
> 4:23–26)

It was during the festival of Passover, that the new saving act of God in Jesus Christ transpired. In this world-changing event of Jesus' death and resurrection, God demonstrated the depth of his love for humanity. Remembrance of Christ's work continues to instill adoration as it attests to God's majestic power and worth. As the love of God is remembered and celebrated, the heart is filled with gratitude, allowing worship to ensue. It is when God's Spirit and our spirits touch that we are truly worshiping. Worship is not something that the church or its leaders have established. God initiated this form of fellowship in order to love, guide, and draw near to humanity. We worship God as we perceive and acclaim his supreme worth and, while in his presence, commit to joining in his work to bring the kingdom of God to earth.

God's nature was consistent throughout the Old and New Testaments. The work of Christ healed our relationship with God and opened the way for the Holy Spirit to enter our lives. This feat not only expanded our understanding of God but apprised us of his will for us and awakened our response to his worthiness. Jesus reminds us that the commandments have not changed. Jesus tells us the first commandment continues to be "the Lord is one; you shall love the Lord your God with all your heart, and with all your soul, and with all your mind, and with all your strength" (Mark 12:29b–30). Further, Jesus includes a second commandment, "You shall love your neighbor as yourself. There is no other commandment greater than these." (Mark 12:31b). A scribe agreed with Jesus and added that these two commandments are "much more important than all whole burnt offerings and sacrifices" (Mark 12:33b). To which Jesus replied to the scribe, "You are not far from the kingdom of God" (Mark 12:34b).

The sacrifices and burnt offerings of the Old Testament are no longer necessary, and there is no longer an ancestral distinction among God's people. Everyone is in the family of God, and there is fresh emphasis on loving your neighbor as yourself. This fellowship and mutual service toward each other is the sacrifice which God desires. As we worship in spirit, we perceive God's design for humanity more clearly and are empowered and equipped to participate in bringing it to the world through our service of loving neighbor as self. The pattern of worshiping God and participating in building God's kingdom becomes a continuous and all-encompassing sphere in which we are to live. This rhythm is how a life of worship flows. Paradoxically, while in a time of worship we also sense just how far we are from loving as God loves, but at the same time we become empowered in God's strength to love others as he does. As we increasingly grasp the immensity of God's creation and love for humanity, our worship deepens.

Assembled for Worship

As individuals, we engage in a life of worship. But we also regularly gather as a faith community to remember whom we worship, jointly enter the presence of God, and together contribute to the *why* of worship by participating in spreading God's kingdom throughout the world. As we now begin to look at what activities we include as we gather, we need to remain aware of the distinction between a worship service and worship. A service of worship leads the gathered people into worship. Attendance at the service does not guarantee that worship will occur.

Early Development of Worship Services

For millennia God's people have gathered to experience worship centered around the tabernacle, temple, and synagogues, with practices that included scripture reading and interpretation. Indeed, Jesus joined in synagogue activities during his time on earth. Through his teachings, both in the synagogues and in public gatherings, he informed the people of his divine identity and that he had come to earth to fulfill God's promise of salvation. But not all believed Jesus to be the long-awaited savior. People began to separate into those who believed in Jesus as the Messiah and those who were still waiting for a messiah, and they began to meet apart from each other. Since many of these early Christians, as they were beginning to be called, had previously been associated with the synagogues, it is no surprise that their meetings adopted similar approaches in how they conducted their services of worship. They continued to sing, praise, pray, and read from the Old Testament scriptures. But they also read manuscripts which would later become the New Testament. These letters and documents informed the assembled people of God's saving act in Jesus Christ and what this revelation meant for their lives. The sacraments of baptism and the Lord's Supper, both with roots in Jesus' teachings, began to be celebrated in these meetings. Also, the reciting of affirmations of their beliefs took place in this time of gathered worship. They might incorporate a statement as simple as *Jesus is Lord,* or more lengthy hymn-style passages might be used to expound the events of Christ, such as we now find in Philippians 2:6–11 or 1 Timothy 3:16. These early gatherings of Christians began in homes, but later the gathering places became more permanent, from simple one-room churches to massive cathedrals.

The New Testament specifies no definitive pattern for a community's worship service. However, the simplified version of the early development of Christian worship services presented above demonstrates how a collection of elements began to come together. Over time churches included various elements of worship found in the New Testament and interpreted, blended, adapted, and finally authorized them in their particular *books of worship.* These books of worship outline the patterns for services for a variety of situations, including weekly worship, weddings, and funerals, as well as the liturgy for the sacraments. The various services often incorporate a variety of elements, but generally include song, prayer, praise, affirmation of beliefs, scripture reading, sacraments, and instruction in the faith.

Later Developments of Worship Services

With no definitive biblical instruction for how to conduct a worship service, many forms and styles have developed. Diverse forms continue to develop as cultures transform, changing the context in which the service takes place. In the last few decades the change has been rapid, creating many challenges for congregations and worship leaders. Leaders of worship services walk a fine line as they plan *how* the service will unfold. They must guide the people to remember *who* God is and *why* they worship, while at the same time becoming invisible, making room for Christ, through the Holy Spirit, to lead the worshipers.

Worship cannot be molded into a human construct; the Holy Spirit cannot simply be apprehended, nor can it be organized or institutionalized without the risk of suffocating it. In designing a worship service, the goal is to seek the extraordinary experience of God's presence for those who have gathered. True spiritual worship wells up when the spirit of the individual and the Holy Spirit connect. Therefore, the worship service is to lay the groundwork and prepare the people to intentionally give the Holy Spirit access to their hearts.

Worship, that is, spirit touching Spirit, goes beyond enjoying a euphoric experience of forgiveness, restoration, and awe; it also includes accepting responsibility and accountability in carrying out one's role in expanding the kingdom of God. During a time of worship, God empowers worshipers to identify and carry out their part in transforming acts within their community and the world. These gathered communities, or congregations, come together to achieve for God what an individual alone could not. Taken together, these gathered individuals, blessed with diverse gifts, become one body in Christ. Together they contribute toward bringing God's kingdom to earth.

I believe all faithful worship leaders have a goal of leading people into the presence of God, but their idea of how this task is best accomplished can differ greatly, as can the context in which they lead. There has never been a one-size-fits-all worship style, neither in New Testament times nor the present day. Perhaps we put too much emphasis on the *how* of worship. I have studied the proliferation of books and participated in countless conversations on the various styles of worship services and reasons for the need to adapt to changing times. I have led contemporary as well as traditional services and am aware of the magnitude of this issue. However, the issue is not which style is better; there are strengths and weaknesses to each. And it is true that people have a natural tendency and a history of cherished customs which draw them to a particular style of worship service. I confess, given a choice, I'm more comfortable in a traditional service. Although there is something of a need to adapt the style and form of worship services to fit the culture and preferences of the gathered people, we need not overindulge potential worshipers.

God taught me a valuable lesson when we moved to a Muslim country in the Middle East. There were only three locations where Christian worship services were allowed—one Protestant, one Catholic, and one Orthodox. The Protestant congregation, which I participated in, consisted of persons from over sixty nations. I was engulfed in a sea of diversity. The worship services were about as far from the style of a North American traditional service as you could find. The only commonalities were that Jesus Christ was the one worshiped and the language was English. At first, I struggled to find the presence of God in this unfamiliar setting. Had there been another choice for community worship, one more in-line with my preferences, I am certain I would have moved to it. But there was no other choice, and God led me to the beauty of his presence in this diverse group of people. I was shown how their unfamiliar ways could bring me even deeper into his presence. I came to appreciate their unique customs, vociferous worship, and alternate approaches to theology. I was not in agreement with all aspects of the church's affairs. But we had the love of Christ in common and that unity proved enough. It is agreement in the *who* and *why* of worship that holds a congregation together. It is unfortunate that the issue of worship service style, the *how* of worship, has created such divisiveness and distraction. As long as we let this and other institutional church issues persist to divide us, the weaker the gathered church becomes and the less able we are in realizing the harmony God desires.

In America our freedom to repeatedly move to a congregation that is more to our liking not only prevents us from enjoying the beautiful diversity in humanity but diminishes the diversity of spiritual gifts within a congregation. The diversity of gifts or blessings that each individual receives and brings to the gathered group contributes to the unity of the body of Christ and growth of the kingdom of God. God does not always put us in the place that best fits our comfort zone, but he will fit us comfortably into where we find ourselves.

It is not the form of worship that is important, but the transformation of the heart during worship that is paramount. The expression of worship may take the form of silence and stillness or shouts of praise and joy. It can take place anytime and anywhere, whether one is alone or in a gathered fellowship. It may embody symbols and metaphors in order to express God's all-powerful and loving nature when ordinary words fail. Any service of worship that is focused on Jesus Christ with attention to God's truth and grace can lead the people into the presence of God. As worship deepens and we are overwhelmed by God's love, it translates into a passionate response of conformity to God's will which blesses the world.

8

Doubt: Can Faith Coexist with Doubt?

SWEPT UP IN THE excitement of Easter celebrations with sounding trumpets, fragrant lilies, and a mass of celebrants—a surge of assurance moves over the gathered crowds. This public witness to faith in Christ's resurrection gives rise to a veracious scene. However, no sooner has the last *alleluia* been sung than life's routines return and the whole idea of the resurrection of Christ may start to fade or seem ridiculously incredible. Thomas, one of Jesus' twelve disciples, reflects on the intrusion of doubt which resonated within his rational mind:

> Thomas . . . said to them [the other disciples], "Unless I see the mark of the nails in his [Jesus'] hands, and put my finger in the mark of the nails and my hand in his side, I will not believe." (John 20:24–25)

The story of doubting Thomas is scheduled to be read on the Sunday following Easter by churches all over the world. This timing is unfortunate because the story of this honest skeptic, which addresses a very important aspect of faith—doubt—will be heard by only a small portion of the throngs that were present for Easter. The Sunday after Easter is *low Sunday*, so named for its prevalent lack of attendance. In season or out of season, an understanding of the troublesome yet inevitable co-existence of faith and doubt begs to be addressed. Jesus' disciples, whom we meet in scripture, have left us with many illustrations of the role doubt played within their faith journeys.

Those Without Doubt

For those who believe they have no doubts concerning their Christian faith, I would encourage caution. Some faith communities create an atmosphere that discourages doubt. Within these communities some individuals can be uncomfortable exploring or admitting their doubts. Many earnest, but perhaps overzealous, Christian leaders promote convictions which do not accommodate doubt. This approach can lead to pitfalls of a legalistic nature, where strict adherence to institutional requirements are emphasized rather than giving attention to each individual's unique path to faith. Legalistic approaches set up external measures to evaluate faith. Such legalisms might include arbitrary attendance and membership requirements, or one may feel pressured to profess beliefs before they understand or accept them. The moment we begin to pretend we believe in order to meet some measurable standard is the moment we begin to hinder our growth. Legalism creates a way to externally manage and control but leaves little room for the exploration that is necessary in matters of faith. The result is to reduce faith to norms that spring more from cultural and social pressures than Christian ideals.

When, for whatever reason, one does not feel safe expressing doubt, an unwillingness to explore and search for truth sets in. Doubt then becomes smothered with Christian clichés and jargon that turn faith into nothing more than superficial zeal. Doubts need to be authentically owned, just as faith needs to be authentically owned. It is a little ironic, but I often observe that when a Christian is in church, they feel they must deny their doubts, but when in public they often tend to downplay their Christian beliefs. Cultural and social pressures wield subtle but strong influences in our lives. No wonder we can be confused over what we do and do not believe.

Faith and Doubt Defined

In approaching the subject of the coexistence of faith and doubt, we need to put forth a few definitions. The subjects in which we can have faith are boundless, but in the case of this chapter, as already implied, we will address faith associated with Christian beliefs. But we should probably keep in mind that Christians are not the only ones with doubts. Atheists and agnostics also have doubts. Consider the committed choir member who shows up and performs beautifully to the glory of God—just in case it is all true. Their singing is simultaneously a statement of faith and doubt, even if they do not realize it.

"Faith" is such an overused word that it has almost lost any meaning. Its synonym "belief" is just as vague. One author has suggested that the biblical meaning of faith can be expressed with more clarity as *God-confidence*.[1] Confidence is an easier concept to grasp than faith. With this definition questions such as, "Do you have faith in God, the Bible, or Jesus Christ?" become, "How strong is your confidence that God exists, that the scriptures contain truth, that Jesus was divine, and that the Holy Spirit is present with us now?" Along these same lines, doubt can simply be thought of as a lack of confidence. Our confidence (faith) and lack of confidence (doubt) are a response to what we know and how confident we are in what we know.

What Do We Know?

How we acquire knowledge is addressed by an entire branch of philosophy, called epistemology, which has its roots at least as far back as the fifth century BC when hypothesized by Greek philosophers Socrates and Plato. Without wading through all the philosophical arguments, epistemology deals with how we know something, how we attain knowledge, and how certain we are that we know something. As it turns out, it is remarkable to know anything with absolute certainty, especially if it is not about an object that our senses can inspect, such as an apple that we can see, touch, taste, smell, or hear drop from a tree. Even though Socrates conjectured extensively about how we know something, he shied away from claiming that we can know anything with 100 percent certainty.

Some beliefs defy measurement and cannot be scientifically proven. We justify such beliefs by collecting an overwhelming amount of evidence that gives us confidence they are true. Indeed, there are many things we know but cannot prove. For example, we cannot prove that our pets have feelings, but we believe they do. We believe our dogs love us when they settle into our laps. We believe they are happy when we pet them and they wag their tails. Their reactions are the evidence we collect in order to have confidence that they have feelings. Many of the things we think we know are conclusions developed strictly from overwhelming evidence.

Returning to Thomas, his first evidence toward believing in Jesus Christ's resurrection was that the other disciples told him they had seen Jesus after his death.

> Jesus came and stood among them . . . he showed them his hands and his side . . . But Thomas . . . was not with them when

1. Moreland and Issler, *Search of a Confident Faith*, 9.

Jesus came. So the other disciples told him, "We have seen the Lord." (from portions of John 20:19–20, 24–25)

Thomas, although familiar with these other reliable disciples, still doubted what they told him. He could not believe unless he had seen Jesus for himself. Hearing from the other disciples was second-hand evidence; he needed more to reasonably justify this belief. The story continues:

> A week later his [Jesus'] disciples were again in the house, and Thomas was with them. Although the doors were shut, Jesus came and stood among them and said, "Peace be with you." Then he said to Thomas, "Put your finger here and see my hands. Reach out your hand and put it in my side. Do not doubt but believe." Thomas answered him, "My Lord and my God!" Jesus said to him, "Have you believed because you have seen me? Blessed are those who have not seen and yet have come to believe." (John 20:26–29)

Thomas finally had enough evidence to believe that Jesus was alive. How great it would be to encounter evidence as conclusive as Thomas enjoyed. Today, however, our confidence rests in a large part on the evidence of the witnesses of long ago. For Thomas, his belief—knowing, confidence, trust, however we want to think of faith—was a process of accumulating evidence. Even Jesus' reference to those who "have come to believe" implies there is a process in developing a confident faith. Perhaps, like Thomas, we struggle with a need for more tangible proof. The mixture of doubt and faith creates an unsettled atmosphere that calls out for more validation.

Biblical accounts are one source of evidence that contribute to our confidence in a belief. However, for some, the object of their doubt includes the credibility of the scriptures. Fortunately, there are other sources to employ. In addition to biblical witnesses, we can engage reliable contemporary witnesses, hear their testimonies, and discuss their understandings. Our own experiences are added to the mix as well, including revelation that we may be graced with, which will be discussed shortly. We ease our doubt and gain confidence in a belief by acquiring more knowledge. Gaining knowledge is a continuous process that involves the collection of information, the investigation of evidence, and the formulation of conclusions. Once we are satisfied with the validity of the evidence and the conclusions, we can let this piece of new knowledge contribute toward strengthening our faith. Our faith is a response to the strength of confidence in our knowledge.

Spiritual Knowing

We love order and clarity. Our acquisition of knowledge is fed by reason, experience, biblical witness, and contemporary testimonies, as well as our five senses. We submit much of life, including Christian beliefs, to reason and highly developed rational arguments. However, religious beliefs rarely lend themselves to being solely proven with logic. We cannot speak of the resurrection of Christ as if it were rational. Attempts to explain the resurrection with reason, perhaps by making it a metaphor, trivialize its significance. Leaving behind our engrained dependence on reason and embracing what cannot be seen is a recognition that there is more to humanity than can be intellectually explained. For some, this parting with rationalization is difficult. Although our minds have been created with the capacity for rational thought, it is also plausible to reach for truth that does not come via logic.

The possibility exists to receive special revelation or knowledge in our spirit. This experience would be like that of John Wesley when he disclosed, "I felt my heart strangely warmed. I felt I did trust Christ . . . an assurance was given me."[2] Many persons have had experiences that added to their knowledge concerning God's existence and activity in our world through revelation. This often comes during biblical study, as in Wesley's case, or during prayer. But what is even more astounding and promising is that God can surprise us with his voice of assurance at any moment.

In the act of rationalization, we are usually listening to only our own voice. When we open ourselves to the possibility of hearing God's voice, we cultivate a heart that can distinguish God's voice from ours. Doubts provide openings that place us before God's grace. This grace can stimulate a passion in us to hear that distant voice and encourage us to leave our own voice behind as we go in search of new knowledge and confidence.

Faith and Doubt Cycle

But even for John Wesley, doubt hung around after his heart was strangely warmed. We learn from his writings that his moment of revelation was important to him throughout his life, but it did not eliminate all questions.[3] He continued to seek and acquire knowledge to alleviate his doubts. Other giants of faith that have acknowledged their doubts were Martin Luther, C. S. Lewis, and Mother Teresa.[4] We see this kind of vacillation in scripture

2. Heitzenrater, *Mirror and Memory*, 106.
3. Heitzenrater, *Mirror and Memory*, 106–7.
4. Young, *Room for Doubt*, 94, 98, 105.

as well. Consider the following passage. This story illustrates that the Bible bears witness that our faith will waver. Whether we interpret this story as a rending of the natural laws or as metaphorical in essence, it gives us a window into the nature of doubt in a faithful disciple.

> Peter answered him, "Lord, if it is you command me to come to you on the water." He said, "Come." So Peter got out of the boat, started walking on the water, and came toward Jesus. But when he noticed the strong wind, he became frightened, and begin-ning to sink, he cried out, "Lord, save me!" Jesus immediately reached out his hand and caught him, saying to him, "You of little faith, why did you doubt?" When they got into the boat, the wind ceased. And those in the boat worshiped him, saying, "Truly you are the Son of God." (Matt 14:28–33)

Peter vacillated between faith and doubt. His first statement, "*if* it is you," expresses doubt. Then faith was required to step out of the boat. However, doubt re-emerged as he was distracted by the storm, and he began to sink. His return to faith is seen in his asking the Lord to save him. Our minds strive to eliminate ambiguity. We think we must have complete faith, or we have no faith. But such certainty is rarely the norm in real life. When waves crash around us and we are clinging to the boat, our most resolute faith may begin to dissolve. But honestly, doubt simply confirms that we are already venturing down the road of faith.

Peter demonstrated to us the process we are to follow. Faith is not about always being able to walk on water, but rather is about being able to bring our doubts to God. When the storm began to overwhelm Peter, he cried out "Lord, save me!" While we do not have Jesus physically standing before us as Peter did, the living Christ is just as available to us through prayer. When our security disintegrates, we can make the wonderful discovery that the God of our unsteady faith is steadfastly there.

Faith, like life, is often a series of ups and downs. Peter again gives us examples of the process one goes through in establishing firm beliefs as we observe him wavering between trust and doubt. In Matthew 16:16 Peter de-clares Jesus to be the Messiah. A few verses later in Matthew 16:22–23 Peter misunderstands Jesus' mission and is seen as a stumbling block to Jesus' purposes. In Matthew 26:33 Peter tells Jesus, "I will never desert you." Only a short while later, in Matthew 26:72, Peter says of Jesus, "I do not know the man." However, over time Peter added to his faith as he walked with Je-sus, with every step acquiring evidence and discarding doubts. Throughout scripture we can observe Peter's confidence growing, and by the time we get to his sermon in Acts 2, we see that he, after receiving the Holy Spirit, has gained much confidence in his beliefs. An examination of Peter's life confirms for us that faith does not develop in a straight line.

Summary

I hope this chapter has lightened the burden for anyone who feels a lack of confidence in their faith. The road to growth in faith is one that each person must walk independently, for our unique life experiences leave us with a distinct medley of doubts. Confidence in Christian beliefs is a unique challenge because it does not happen in the same way we progress in job proficiency or in academic work. We cannot see or measure the inner workings of our spirit in the same way we can move through the ranks in our careers or obtain degrees. Although we can engage tangibles such as scripture and testimonies of witnesses to feed our rational minds, we must also allow our less perceptible, more spiritual nature to engage other approaches. These avenues are activated through prayer, listening, and a general expectant openness to the activity of God in our lives. We may experience gradual confidence or may be blessed with a sudden and profound event. Momentary, life-changing spiritual experiences can happen, but even when they do, they are not the end of one's journey. Not only can questions remain, but new circumstances will enter our lives, bringing with them new doubts or a return of old ones. This state is not an unseemly one, but rather the normal condition of one in pursuit of faith. The words of Mark 9:24 confirm with clarity that faith and doubt are not mutually exclusive: "I believe; help my unbelief!" Having the courage to face our doubts is truly, although ironically, a strong statement of faith.

9

Prayer: Does it Change Anything?

THE TREMENDOUS NUMBER OF books that have been written about prayer attests to both the importance and the perceived complexity of this spiritual practice. The aspects that these books cover are endless, and I will *not* attempt to address the entire field. The bulk of this chapter will deal with the most frequently repeated questions concerning prayer during my pastoral ministry. I believe these inquiries reveal the issues that are the most common hurdles to deepening an individual's prayer life.

We have come to depend on measurable observations to engage in and comprehend our world. As a result, the abstract conveyance of prayer can be mystifying. Adding to the mystery is the tangled mass of motives and psychological issues that often accompany us into prayer. Restlessness, fear, or a search for meaning prompt many prayers, while gratitude and thankfulness inspire prayer at other times. Regardless of the circumstances that turn us toward prayer, the predominant impetus is the realization that we are not as autonomous as we often perceive ourselves to be. This acceptance of our vulnerability is the beginning of engagement with God. In fact, a basic definition of prayer is simply *engagement with God.*

Although the definition of prayer is simple, how the encounter happens is rather ambiguous. Engagement with God often does not follow the expectations of a pragmatist nor satisfy the contemplative sentimentalist. The encounter may resemble a struggle, or the experience may feel more like a close friendship. It may bring with it more questions or it may move one to a deep understanding that has been elusive in the past. The inexplicable nature of prayerful engagement coupled with the movement it produces in one's life can be perplexing. We want to know how prayer *works*, but that is not within our grasp. Adding to incomprehensibility of how prayer works is the fact that an authentic experience with God requires us to relinquish control of the outcome.

Distinctiveness of Christian Prayer

Prayer begins in our thoughts; we sometimes refer to this as meditation. Christian prayer is a form of meditation, but not all meditation is Christian prayer. Neither are our meditations Christian prayer simply because they have a noble goal. A non-Christian could equally be meditating on a virtuous goal. Neither is meditation ensured to be Christian prayer because the one praying professes the Christian faith. Christians can practice forms of meditation that are outside of Christian prayer, such as yoga, to improve their health as they exercise their body. There is no attempt to lose oneself or float away from reality during prayer, but rather both the head and heart are employed to receive God's grace.

One distinctiveness of Christian prayer is reflected in the often-spoken words, *in Jesus name I pray.* This phrase is repeated so often that there is potential for its meaning to become inconsequential and offered with emptiness. But these words take us to the very heart of Christian prayer. They summon a recollection of the entire achievements of Jesus, expressing confidence that he has opened and provides the way for our intimate communication with God. Christ has brought into the world and our individual lives the possibility for change and restoration through prayer.

Although one enters prayer in stark barrenness with all pretense stripped away, one does not enter with a blank slate. There are always some elements that the individual brings into their time of prayer. These elements are of utmost importance. One is reminded of the old computer cliché, "Garbage in, garbage out." If what goes into meditation is not good and true, what comes out will not be any better. The Christian seeks to take in truth, including truth about themselves, their situation, a worldly state of affairs, or truth from scripture. Letting the words of scripture come alive by giving the Holy Spirit free reign with one's meditation is a time-honored practice which has borne fruit throughout the ages. For example, if it is peace one is seeking, then one might take the words of Jesus, "My peace I give to you," into one's meditation. In this meditation one may realize what is hindering their peace, that Christ's peace is accessible, and that they are invited to become a part of that peace.

The long history of Christian meditation and the various techniques employed reflect the widespread yearning to discover God's presence in the midst of prayer. It is a hope-filled venture. The hope is not to feel a momentary high, although this may well be experienced. Christian meditation includes the confident and heartening expectation that individuals and the world will be enriched through God's response during prayerful listening. You may even realize that you can be the answer to someone else's prayer.

There Are No Rules

A common hinderance to one's prayer life is a lack of confidence born from the fear that one may not be praying *correctly*. The good news is that there are no secret handshakes and no rules that initiate or embody prayerful communication with God. Superficial approaches such as body posture or the position of the hands are not of great import. Likewise, there is no particular building or place that makes prayer more effective. It is even acceptable to fall asleep while praying. There is no better evidence of putting your trust in the holy presence of God than falling asleep. And if you worry about not making a special time for prayer in your frantic schedule, well, that is a prayer in itself.

It is important to be free of insubstantial rules or imposed traditions that distract from being confident in one's prayer life. Some guidelines for prayer may have served a good purpose in the past but now frustrate authentic prayer. Bowing one's head and closing one's eyes, while helpful at times, is not a requirement. Many gardeners have spent hours weeding and planting while praying in mantra-like fashion with eyes wide open during this repetitive task. Each person must evaluate their experiences, eliminating practices which do not inspire prayer and retaining those that do.

In addition to rules and traditions, there should be similar *un*concern regarding the pious use of sacramental words. Although there are many books of beautiful liturgical prayers which have their place in our prayer life, overdependence on these can cause one to avoid uniquely frank and plain-spoken conversations with God that need to happen. The disciples asked Jesus to teach them to pray, to which Jesus replied with what we refer to as the Lord's Prayer (Matt 6:9–13). This extraordinary prayer leads many into a conversation with God and teaches us much about prayer. It is good to learn from the master teacher, and the words of this and other special prayers are wonderful *if* we affirm their meaning while reciting them. But when repetition dulls the power of a prayer, its recitation can become the "heaped up empty phrases" that Jesus warns of in Matthew 6:7. There are no magical incantations; prayer is a sincere and open-hearted conversation with God. We can be completely candid in our prayers, for God can be trusted to move us in the direction of our best interest.

It is also important to remember that the titles people hold, such as reverend, chaplain, or pastor, do not make their prayers more effective than those of the untitled. Although the overtures of those who have put in the study to earn their degrees and associated titles may help one enter into prayer, a complete diet of others' prayers on one's behalf can preclude an essential and veracious conversation with God. God's concern goes beyond external and outward considerations and attends to the passion, earnestness, and disposition of the one who has occasion for prayer.

We can confidently enter into a prayerful conversation with God, eliminating any anxiousness about not praying *correctly* because the only *wrong* way is to not pray at all. As Romans 8:26 reminds us, "The Spirit helps us in our weakness; for we do not know how to pray as we ought, but that very Spirit intercedes with sighs too deep for words." Prayer is not dependent on outward rules or words; it transpires in the spirit.

Understanding the Response

I have been concentrating on our part in prayer, but it is God's momentous response that is the crucial aim. God's response to our prayer is found after we stop talking and listen with our heart and spirit. That is how this conversation is accomplished. In today's world, active expression seems more acceptable and laudable than imperceptible listening. But it is in the listening that new direction is imparted. Prayer that is approached in faith and accompanied with a passive listening heart leaves one ready to hear God's words of hope and transformation.

We sometimes hear people exclaim their *prayer has been answered* or that *prayer works*. What do they mean by these statements? If these phrases are being used to express that someone simply *got what they wanted*, then it is possible prayer is being trivialized and misunderstood as a tool for self-indulgence. The one praying may be assuming that they alone know what they need. However, if these simple words are used because no vocabulary exists which can accurately describe the amazing and awesome work of God in their lives, then prayer is being recognized for its true breadth and splendor.

It is often the discomfort that we feel but cannot quite identify which prods us to approach prayer. It is God's responding grace that untangles our thoughts and births hope when praying at these times. God's grace finds us and touches our spirit as we look for answers in prayer. A new and assured vision of life can be the response to these prayers. It is faith in God's love for us that allows us to trust and act on that new vision. Prayer is the means of grace that gives us hope beyond the present situation and allows us to move toward what might be. Such hope is what we can expect when we pray.

Prayer Without Answers

But what if we pray and fail to perceive a response? Do some prayers go unanswered? That is a genuine and deeply perplexing question that cannot be swept under the rug. Many have read the promise in Mark 11:24, "So I tell you, whatever you ask for in prayer, believe that you have received it, and it will be yours." There are other similar promises in Matthew 7:7–8, "Ask, and it will be given you; search, and you will find; knock, and the door will be opened for you. For everyone who asks receives, and everyone who searches finds, and for everyone who knocks, the door will be opened." John 15:7 and 14:12–14 also speak of such receiving. All these passages dwell uneasily in the mind of those who have prayed faithfully for a loved one to be healed, for a child to return home, for a job, or for some desperate need on the world's stage, only to stand by as none of these commendable petitions come to pass.

Some reasons offered for unanswered prayer fall on one's ears like the insensitive and unsound comments of Job's friends explaining why he lost everything. Such comments might include a suggestion that the one praying lacks enough faith. The fact that a prayer has been lifted in the first place invalidates this reason. Then there are those who box in God's responses to three options; *yes, no*, and *wait*, suggesting that the lack of an answer means the response was either *no* or *have more patience*. This thinking feigns an oversimplification of the complexities in life as well as misses the depth and sincerity that transpires during engagement with God.

Other grasping reasons offered for not receiving what we petition God for include the potential that from where we stand, we cannot see the entire picture, or that what we ask may not be in our best interest, or it may be detrimental to someone else, or perhaps we do not yet have the maturity to receive what we ask for. Contradictive prayers are also conceivable. Consider that two persons of equal qualifications apply for the same job. Both are in similar need of employment and both faithfully pray to be hired. One of these prayers must go unanswered in the sense of gaining employment. However, the answer to a prayer is more than receiving what we ask for.

The deeper meaning of prayer involves developing an authentic relationship with God through a genuine conversation. Bringing a situation into prayer can have the outcome of bringing clarity to our lives and point us in the right direction. We do not fully understand how prayer *works* and are sometimes puzzled by the *outcome*. Even so, it is important to continue the conversation with God that we began.

A Testimony of Prayer with No Answer

My hometown, with a population over one hundred thousand, experienced an extended time of unanswered prayer. Our region entered a severe drought in 2010. By 2011 the drought intensified with more than one hundred days of temperatures over one hundred degrees. The lack of rain coupled with the hot, dry air accelerated the evaporation of the lake which contained the city's source of water. Signs that read "Pray for Rain" popped up in front of homes throughout the city. The rain did not come. Prayer however, remained a fuel for hope. The city leaders publicly joined in asking the citizens to pray. Worship services throughout town regularly included prayers for rain.

God often calls for our cooperation to bring our prayers to fruition. The people faithfully came together to reduce water consumption by more than 45 percent, cloud seeding was unsuccessfully attempted, a failed attempt was made to cover the lake with a substance to prevent evaporation, sewer water was cleaned and returned for drinking, ingenious systems were developed to collect what little rain did fall, and buckets of grey water from the homes were used to save a few struggling plants. However, the drought continued. Years passed. By 2015 jobs were being lost, people were moving away, livestock were being sold, and businesses were closing. With less than a year's worth of water left in the lake the situation was dire. The extended weather forecasts gave no signs of hope. The Pray for Rain signs were faded and brittle from the hot sun. People stood together praying in the dry, cracked lake bed. Still no rain. *What were we to think but that our prayers had gone unanswered?*

Then, in May of 2015, five years after the drought began, the rains came in torrents and drenched the lake's watershed. With a few weeks of unprecedented rainfall, the lake filled beyond capacity. I cannot begin to imagine how many prayers petitioned for rain during those five years. We will likely never know why the rains ceased or why they returned. It is true that prayer is about our communication and relationship with God and not about receiving what we ask for. But we cannot deny the paradox that while scripture encourages us to express our needs to God, they are not always realized.

Over the next weeks a steady stream of people made their way out to the lake to see its astounding return. They were drawn to the spillway to watch the water go over the top. They just stood there—mostly in silence—watching the water flow. Perhaps for many who had prayed, these were intimate moments with God. Such intimate moments are the pinnacle of prayer—a shared encounter that requires no action and needs no words.

Expectations of Prayers for Healing

One of the most frequent prayers is a plea for the restoration of physical or mental health for oneself or a loved one, so I would like to address this prayer separately. Even though we know we are not promised unending health and mortality is inevitable, the thought of losing our health even temporarily is dismaying. A lack of health instills an unease born of the vulnerability and loss of independence illness can bring. Although we are encouraged to pray at all times and in all situations, the precariousness of one's health and loss of control is frequently the tipping point that sends us into prayer. Prayers for healing carry with them the uncertainty between restored health or continued illness. But they also bring with them the possibility of turning our suffering into courage and peaceful acceptance of our situation, diminishing the agitation caused by the loss of health.

This outcome does not keep us from praying for a complete cure, even when the odds are against us. Miraculous healings are recounted in the scriptures. Additionally, there are documented cases throughout history. During my hospital ministry I witnessed healings that could not be scientifically explained and were attributed to prayer. However, these are still the exceptions and we have no firm explanation for the seemingly sporadic and unpredictable nature of these healings. Medical science remains a gift God has given us that is most often responsible for curing illness today.

So why are a few people healed miraculously while others progress in the medically expected manner? This question has no answer. However, the miracles of physical healing that we are occasionally graced with give one further assurance of God's active presence and affirm one's faith. But at the same time, we are reminded that the complete reign of God is yet to come, and we continue to pray, "Thy kingdom come, thy will be done on earth as it is in heaven." Our faith will not always bless us with physical healing. Moreover, we live in the certainty that we will all eventually experience the death of our earthly bodies. So, you might ask, "Why then do we pray for physical healing?"

It is through prayer that we are nurtured in our relationship with God. Although prayer for healing will not necessarily result in a cure, it will open a place where one can receive new strength and courage. God's power is just as much present in suffering as it is in healing. While miraculous healing affirms our faith, we find no less affirmation in the person who experiences God's comfort in a time of suffering.

We continue to pray for healing because we believe in a God who has the power to heal and these prayers are an act of compassion which in itself can lead to healing. We are repeatedly made aware of Jesus' compassion preceding healing. Take note of the words *compassion*, *mercy*, and *pity* in the following verses. Matthew 14:14 recounts, "When he [Jesus] went ashore, he saw a great crowd; and he had compassion for them and cured their sick." In the story of the good Samaritan (Luke 10:29–37), the Samaritan was "moved with pity" and bandaged the man's wounds. Jesus later commends this Samaritan who "showed mercy" to the wounded man. In Luke 7:13 we are told Jesus "had compassion" for the widow and healed her son. In Mark 5:19 Jesus "showed mercy" to the demonic in healing him. In Mark 1:41 Jesus was "moved with pity" before he healed the leper. And in Matthew 20:34 Jesus was "moved with compassion" as he touched the blind and restored their sight. Prayer for healing is vital because it is an act of compassion which gives and sustains hope.

Does Prayer Change Anything?

This chapter has concentrated on prayers of petition and intercession which carry requests to God for oneself or others. We now return to the original question, "Does prayer change anything?" The short answer is, yes. However, the change one expects should not be exclusively understood as receiving what one asks for, even though this may happen. The one who prays can be confident that a conversation with God will change them and thus change the way they live their life. And since we do not live in a vacuum, the change in one's life can very well change the life of another. God does not work alone. The response to our prayers may well culminate in the answer to another's prayer. The changes we can expect to receive while listening for God's responses will not always be tangible, but will include restorative transformations such as insight, wisdom, courage, peace, endurance, forgiveness, and hope, to name a few. We can be confident that prayer sets in motion an audacious journey.

10

Suffering: Why Does God Allow It?

PAIN AND SUFFERING BREAK into our lives; it seems unavoidable. As I sit at my computer to write this chapter, headlines reveal devastating destruction from hurricanes Florence and Michael, while on the other side of the world an earthquake/tsunami combination has swept away thousands of lives in Indonesia. News also arrives of the Las Vegas mass shooting anniversary. One year ago, that rampage resulted in fifty-eight people killed, 413 wounded, and another 456 injured in the resulting confusion. Then news comes of a shooting at a synagogue in Pittsburgh, killing eleven and injuring seven as Shabbat morning services were in progress. These genres of events are all too familiar, leaving a trail of far-reaching uneasy sentiments. In fact, such tragedies now seem so familiar that we are able to predict that the days which follow will be filled with many questions that begin with *why?*

Those were today's headlines. However, the problem of suffering has been with us as far back as we can reach. We need only recall the biblical story of Job or examine the geologic evidence of volcanoes and earthquakes long before recorded history. The memory of lives destroyed at Auschwitz, the constancy of wars, and insidious diseases such as cancer and Alzheimer's serve to remind us that suffering is timeless. There are also contemporary aspects to suffering brought on by our technological advances. We expect our advances to reduce suffering, and they often do. However, they usually also carry the potential for more suffering; for example, nuclear medicine and nuclear bombs, or electricity and environmental decline, or ready access to information on the web and the dark web. And last, but certainly not least, we can add tragic and heartbreaking personal stories that never reach the news.

The recounting of these painful events certainly triggers and validates the *why* questions. Expanding the question further, what if the one who suffers is a theist? Then the problem compounds from *why is there suffering?* into *why does God allow suffering?* It is the theists, the ones who believe in a good God, that are most troubled by the existence of suffering. The problem of pain and suffering in the theistic world is often laid out in some form of the following logic.

1. God is all-knowing (omniscient). God knows what will cause suffering.

2. God is all-powerful (omnipotent). God can act to prevent suffering.

3. God is all-good (omnibenevolent). God does not want us to suffer.

4. Pain and suffering exist.

Therefore, God is either not all-good because God allows suffering, or not all-powerful because God is not able to end suffering. The argument can vary slightly, but the fundamental problem is that, using human logic and reason, one cannot *simultaneously* hold the four statements above as true. However, considered *separately*, Christians and most other theists hold each of the above statements to be true. The question *why does God allow suffering?* therefore begs to be addressed while both recognizing this paradox and maintaining intellectual integrity.

Non-theists are not immune to the pain of suffering and may question why suffering exists, but they can approach the question with less angst, having discarded the expectation of a good and all-powerful God to prevent suffering. To the non-theist, pain and suffering, germs and volcanoes simply exist and there is no need to find a justification for pain congruent with a good God. For many atheists their proof against the existence of God is solely based on the massive evidence of misery in the world. In an ironic sort of way, they have defined their non-existent God as good, one that would not allow suffering. This one phenomenon, the existence of blatant, obtrusive, and egregious suffering, is the most common objection to belief in God and is what causes many believers to subsequently relinquish their faith. The questions that vex a Christian sufferer are so connected with their core belief in a good, loving, and powerful God, that suffering has the potential to morph into a problem of faith. If a theodicy—a rational defense of God's goodness and power in view of the existence of suffering—can be found, it would prevent grievous afflictions from evolving into a dismissal of God, God's goodness, or God's power, as well as ease the pain of the wounded.

The theist has an onerous task to reconcile a good and powerful God within the irrefutable evidence of the enormous extent of human suffering. As the human mind looks for a purpose, a design, a scheme, or anything to make sense of this unwelcomed reality, the search for a theodicy can take on many forms. Persons at various distances from the pain approach the problem differently. The philosopher has the benefit of standing the furthest from the pain—observing, reflecting, and intellectualizing. Then there are the counselors and pastors who must engage the question within the lives of the individuals standing before them, empathizing with each sufferer. And still closer to the pain are friends and relatives of the one who suffers. But the sufferers, no matter how many people surround them, often stand apart, lost in their thoughts and bereft of a way forward.

Search for a Theodicy

Let us begin the search for a theodicy with those farthest from the pain—the theistic philosophers. Using sharp minds, trained in the scientific methods of the Enlightenment, these scholars and thinkers attempt to *reason* an appropriate response to suffering. They do not want their defense of God's goodness to appear simply sentimental, and therefore they seek a rational explanation which often begins with delineating the sources of suffering. The cause of suffering is often referred to as *evil*. Evil in this sense is the general term for something that brings sorrow. The traditional way of identifying the sources of suffering is to distinguish between *moral* evil and *nonmoral* evil. The sins of humankind fall into the category of moral evil and the suffering from natural disasters such as earthquakes fall into non-moral evil.

Sources of Suffering

We begin with the most prominent and easily identified source of suffering—moral evil. It has been estimated that four-fifths of suffering in the world can be attributed to our wrong choices.[1] I do not know how this can be measured, but I think most people would agree that human failings contribute to a large portion of the world's suffering. We have been created with a capacity to freely exercise our will, and in doing so, we have been given the power to make wrong choices—choices which cause us and others to suffer.

---

1. Lewis, *Problem of Pain*, 89.

The freedom to choose our actions is one of the basic attributes of being human. The biblical story of Adam and Eve, an allegory written thousands of years ago, gives an account of humans who right from the beginning exercise their free will as they eat the prohibited fruit. Were they free to choose their actions? Yes. Did God obstruct their freedom? No. Did they make a bad choice? Yes. Did their sin cause suffering? Yes. We humans can burden the world with our bad decisions, sometimes effecting only ourselves, while other times faultless bystanders suffer collateral damage. Saint Augustine (354–430) placed the origin of moral evil wholly in humanity's exercise of free will, leaving God with the ongoing role of redeemer in this damaged world.[2] Additionally, Augustine claimed that the resulting suffering from the misuse of our free will was God's just punishment.[3] Augustine's thesis has enjoyed substantial support over the centuries. Holding up humanity's free will as an explanation for the source of evil is attractive and popular because it extricates God from being the source of evil, keeping God's goodness characteristic intact. It also retains God's attribute of being all powerful because, in preserving our freedom, God is no longer expected to prevent our bad decisions. If God interfered and protected us from our bad decisions, free will would no longer be genuine, and we would simply be puppets on a string. There is no doubt that mistakes born from the misuse of our free will are a large *part* of the breeding ground for suffering. Suffering introduced by our free will, although painful and unwelcome, is at least comprehensible. Make a bad choice, pay the price. Less comprehensible, however, is the suffering of innocents from another's sins.

But is there more to the source of moral evil than our bad decisions? What about the devil or Satan? There is a deafening silence among some Christian denominations on the topic of the demonic. But this topic must be approached if we are to thoroughly address the possible sources of evil. In whatever way we choose to portray the demonic, from an image of a tiny horned devil sitting on our shoulder, or a red figure holding a pitch fork, or an unseen force working to spoil the good in us, we must admit that evil has entered God's creation. Although we cannot say where it comes from, and although it is unseen and unmeasurable, we can open any newspaper and read about evil's engagement in our world. Augustine, however, did not consider evil to have entered creation, but rather considered it to be an *absence* of good, and in attempting to describe this absence he compared it to

2. Augustine, *Confessions*, VII 3, 136.
3. Augustine, *Confessions*, VII 3, 136.

seeing darkness or hearing silence.[4] Although much about the origins of evil is unanswered, there is evidence that humanity experiences evil impulses.

In our humanity we have the ability to respond to thoughts and ideas, both good and bad. You have no doubt heard the phrase, "The devil made me do it." Although this cliché is attractive and convenient for dismissing our responsibility, it is not a valid justification for moral lapses. For whatever the power of evil is, however it arrived and functions on earth, we still have the freedom to make a better choice. Then why do we still make bad choices? This eternal question was emphatically expressed in Romans 7:14–23 as Paul spoke from his inner conflict regarding his freedom to choose: "For I do not do the good I want, but the evil I do not want is what I do" (Rom 7:19). It is a struggle we all face, sometimes with a good outcome and other times, not so much.

When we turn to scripture to elucidate the source of suffering in our world, we remain at a loss for a definitive answer. But what scripture does make clear is that evil, temptation, Satan, or the devil, or however we name it, is in fact an influence opposed to God's will and purposes. To further elucidate the Christian's perception of the demonic, I will briefly expound on three examples from the book of Matthew commonly referenced to validate a demonic force on earth. In Matthew 4:1–11, Jesus, after fasting for forty days, was tempted three times. Each time Jesus responded with scriptural words from the book of Deuteronomy, indicating how these temptations conflicted with God's will, and refused to succumb to the temptation. After the third temptation we hear Jesus say, "Away with you, Satan" (Matt 4:10a). The passage continues, "Then the devil left him" (Matt 4:11a). Jesus was aware of God's will and refused to give into these temptations.

The parable of the wheat and weeds in Matthew 13:24–30 acknowledges that evil, the weeds among the field of good wheat, has indeed invaded our world. The Master of the field is questioned as to where these weeds came from and the Master, God, replies that "an enemy has done this" (Matt 13:28). Further the Master tells the workers of the field to let the wheat and the weeds grow together. This passage informs us that evil is not of God, but is in fact God's enemy, and that the wheat and weeds are difficult to separate, as they endure intertwined together.

This third passage, Matthew 16:21–23, is a conversation between Jesus and Peter in which Jesus is explaining that he will undergo suffering by the elders and chief priests and scribes and be killed. Peter exclaims to Jesus, "This must never happen to you" (Matt 16:22b). At which time Jesus responds to Peter, "Get behind me, Satan!" (Matt 16:23a). Jesus is not saying

4. Augustine, *City of God*, XII 7, 254.

that Peter *is* Satan, but that Peter was offering up a temptation which was against God's will for Jesus.

So far, we have identified sins, our choices outside of God's will, as a source of suffering and recognized that the suffering can extend beyond the one who sinned. And we have allowed the possibility of an unseen outside spiritual force as a source of evil. All these sources of suffering are from moral evil.

Now if we turn to look at non-moral evil, we find that we do not have too much to say. Non-moral evil, things such as earthquakes, floods, and tornadoes, are part of the natural world and are capable of causing a great amount of suffering. Geologic evidence shows they existed long before humans ever came along. But more importantly, we recognize them as independent of human will or actions. Unfortunately, that is about all we can honestly say about experiencing the resultant anguish from the natural processes of our world. Expounding on the sources of suffering has further defined the problem but has not answered *why does God allow suffering?* *Why* questions remain. For what reason or purpose is there suffering? Can we render meaning into suffering which preserves God's good, wise, and powerful characteristics?

Proposed Purposes for Suffering

Many purposes for suffering have been proposed, and I will outline the works of three theistic philosophers. Keep in mind that we are searching for a valid theodicy, an exposition that will find a logical justification for the suffering of humanity while preserving God's attributes of all-knowing, powerful, and loving.

C. S. Lewis remarks that God is giving us pain because he wants to see us remade, but the moment the pain is withdrawn, we go back to our toys.[5] In his proposal, suffering is necessary to develop or mature us, to keep us growing toward what God wants us to be. Such growth could be the outcome on some occasions, but there are just as many painful situations that could cause us to turn away from God. This proposal diminishes God's goodness. For example, how is a child who suffers and dies from cancer, or even worse, at the hand of an abuser, benefitted? I do not see how a good and loving God could cause a child to suffer in this way. The chance for growth cannot justify such inordinate suffering.

Richard Swinburne proposes three reasons that God permits suffering. First, he believes that evil is necessary for persons to learn, through

---

5. Lewis, *Problem of Pain*, 106–7.

experience, to choose right.[6] Admittedly, we do often learn and grow from our experiences, but an experience does not have to include suffering and pain to produce growth. Second, God allows evil so that humans have the opportunity for the noble acts of forgiveness, compassion, and self-sacrifice.[7] And third, God allows enough suffering to occur to bring about some greater good of which we are not aware.[8] The first two reasons offer some legitimate gain from suffering but again fail to keep the good and loving attribute of God intact. For what is good and loving about a God who makes us suffer, and even makes pain *necessary* for moral development? Or what is the use of pain that exists for some reason that is withheld from our understanding, as his third proposal suggests?

One of the most thoroughly considered proposals for a theodicy comes from John Hick and is termed the *Irenaean solution*, so named for his reliance on Irenaeus's theological writings of the second century. Hick questions whether our idea of an ideal creation is the same as God's idea of an ideal creation.[9] Our view of a paradise without pain may conflict with God's view. Hick proposes that in God's ideal creation we are intentionally created imperfect. We are not born pure and then fall into sin, but rather we begin life morally immature and are given opportunities to mature toward our full moral potential through suffering.[10] Hick postulates we are made in God's image but have not yet lived our lives as revealed in Christ, and the suffering of this world is the stage where the process continues.[11] He proposes that through this developmental suffering a future good is being formed, even though we cannot see it, and this future good justifies all the pain.[12] But again, this makes God the author of suffering and belies God's good and loving characteristics. As already mentioned, growth can happen at times as a result of pain and suffering, but there is suffering so cruel and out of proportion to the gain that one cannot imagine how it justifies the end or can be part of an ideal creation. Making suffering *necessary* for developing humanity to maturity simply nullifies the good and loving attribute of God.

In summary, the possible purposes for suffering or attempts to give meaning to our suffering have included variations of the following themes: we suffer because we deserve it as punishment, suffering is necessary to

6. Swinburne, *Existence of God*, 250.

7. Swinburne, *Existence of God*, 240.

8. Swinburne, *Existence of God*, 243.

9. Hick, *Philosophy of Religion*, 44.

10. Hick, *Philosophy of Religion*, 44.

11. Hick, *Philosophy of Religion*, 44.

12. Hick, *Philosophy of Religion*, 47.

develop our altruistic characteristics, suffering is necessary to bring to fruition a bigger plan that we cannot see, suffering is necessary in order for us to grow morally. However, in each of these explanations, the goodness of God is relinquished as soon as suffering is made necessary and conferred any kind of positive meaning or purpose. Making pain necessary nullifies God's goodness and thus nullifies any attempt at a satisfactory theodicy.

The authors of these theories have helped us to understand and define the problem of pain. And occasional truth can be found in their various proposals for conveying meaning to suffering. But none reveal a logical justification for the full extent of the suffering of humanity while simultaneously preserving God's attributes of all-knowing, powerful, and loving. Moreover, these proposals particularly relinquish the goodness of God.

The Sufferer's Way Forward

We must move closer to the pain of those who are immersed in life's troubles if we are to find a way forward. As one author concludes at the end of an entirely analytical book, "The problems posed by the existence of evil have to be more than abstractly analyzed; they have to be lived through and contended with as part of the even more positively mysterious process of human life."[13] The expectations of the philosopher and the sufferer are different, so the way forward is different for each of them. The philosophers want a logical explanation, while the sufferers want to find a way out of the morass that has enveloped them.

When we make this turn from the philosopher's to the sufferer's perspective, what we find is surprising. We paradoxically find that it is the sufferer's viewpoint that most adamantly gives testimony to the goodness of God. While immersed in the pain of suffering, which philosophers contend is necessary, the sufferers are reluctant to recognize any necessity to the extent of their pain. Neither do the suffering find that a theodicy is necessary. However, the sufferer brings a new necessity to the table. The sufferer sees *hope* as *necessary*. And as we will see, sufferers repeatedly find this hope in the guidance of their good God. Another author momentarily relinquished the analytical tone of her book and turned to God for the answer to suffering when she said horrors can "smash Humpty Dumpty so badly that only God can put him back together again."[14]

We can examine the way forward given to us by two well-known authors on this subject, Harold Kushner and Leslie Weatherhead. Harold

13. Kropf, *Evil and Evolution*, 176.
14. Adams, *Horrendous Evils*, 205.

Kushner wrote an excellent book from the viewpoint of the experience of his suffering,[15] and although it has been criticized by the academic world, the academics cannot ignore that this work rings true to experience. The criticism is that it was "written without the benefit of an informed academic exposure to other historical and contemporary theodicies" and that this failing "mars his undeniably significant contribution."[16] Kushner seemed to have expected this criticism, for the opening lines in his book address this issue. He begins his book by letting us know it is written from the perspective of someone close to suffering, the sufferer himself. Kushner even states, "This is not an abstract book about God and theology. It does not try to use big words or clever ways of rephrasing questions . . . This is a very personal book, written by someone who believes in God and in the goodness of the world."[17] Philosophy *speculates* but Kushner *observes*.

Kushner recognizes that there is good and bad in the world and the bad will bring suffering to our lives. Kushner further contends that it is not God that wills us to suffer, but God is available to sustain and comfort us. When we have reached our limits, we can expect new strength from outside of ourselves, from God. Kushner, relating from experience, says that "one of the things that constantly reassures me that God is real . . . is the fact that people who pray for strength, hope, and courage so often find resources of strength, hope, and courage that they did not have before they prayed."[18] Critics of Kushner have argued that in his response to the problem of pain he keeps the all-goodness attribute of God, but not the omnipotence of God.[19] I think Kushner is merely redefining omnipotence. He does not see God as being all-powerful in the sense of being there to control every action, because this would take away free will. However, Kushner's God is all-powerful in the sense of sustaining the individual in all of their circumstances. Again, Kushner gives evidence through experience. He states, "When people who were never particularly strong become strong in the face of adversity, when people who tended to think only of themselves become unselfish and heroic in an emergency, I have to ask myself where they got these qualities which they would freely admit they did not have before. My answer is that this is one of the ways in which God helps us when we suffer beyond the limits of our own strength."[20]

15. Kushner, *When Bad Things Happen*.
16. Whitney, *What Are They Saying*, 76.
17. Kushner, *When Bad Things Happen*, 1.
18. Kushner, *When Bad Things Happen*, 128.
19. Whitney, *What Are They Saying*, 74–75.
20. Kushner, *When Bad Things Happen*, 142.

Weatherhead also writes from a sufferer's viewpoint.[21] He is writing to his congregation in the 1940s during the time of war. He sees a very good God who has an ideal purpose that he describes as God's *intentional will*.[22] Then, in the presence of evil, circumstances appear which give rise to God's *circumstantial will*.[23] This is God's will under less than optimum circumstances. The example he uses out of his historical setting is that a father can be proud that his son is going into the military. However, if the circumstance of the war had never come to be, the father's intentional will might have been that his son go to school and be a doctor. Weatherhead does not answer the question of why there is evil which brings sorrow, but he clearly indicates he does not believe God uses evil to create good. However, the circumstances of evil can reveal good that was already there. For example, war did not make courage, but it often reveals courage that was already there. The third distinction that Weatherhead makes is God's *ultimate will*.[24] This understanding allows us to trust that God's will, ultimately, will be done. That is, in spite of evil, God's goal will be reached with nothing of value lost, thereby illuminating a variation on the definition of omnipotence. God's all-powerful attribute does not mean that everything that happens is God's will, but that nothing can happen that finally defeats God's will. Weatherhead maintains that the *intentional will* of God will *ultimately* be done, even when temporarily interrupted by evil.

Both of these authors, Kushner and Weatherhead, demonstrate a core belief in God's goodness and love as paramount, even as they acknowledge the suffering and pain in this world. Further, they contend that God does not intentionally bring suffering as a way of punishing or molding us. These authors show an understanding of God's omnipotence as constrained, in the sense that God will not manipulate particular circumstances. But God's power is not constrained, as it lovingly provides individuals the strength to sustain them in their anguish. From the experience of these sufferers, we learn that our best response to suffering is to face it with the expectant hope of receiving the strength, courage, and comfort that God will provide.

There is no reason to be naïve, to be idealistic, or to underestimate the power of suffering; we must grieve our losses. But for the Christian, the *necessary* ingredient of *hope* is real and is just as real as the suffering. Hope allows us to see through new eyes, freeing us from the relentlessness and oppression of the present situation and propelling us forward toward

21. Weatherhead, *Will of God*.
22. Weatherhead, *Will of God*, 14.
23. Weatherhead, *Will of God*, 14.
24. Weatherhead, *Will of God*, 15.

a future of new possibilities. Kushner and Weatherhead have been authentic witnesses to suffering, as have many whom I have had the privilege of walking alongside in ministry experiences. It is these true-to-life reliable witnesses and ambassadors of the power of hope in God that validate the way out of the mire of suffering. There is a familiar passage in the Bible that expresses this assurance. The context of the passage is one of encouragement to rise above sorrowful moments. It reads, "But those who wait for the Lord shall renew their strength, they shall mount up with wings like eagles, they shall run and not be weary, they shall walk and not faint" (Isa 40:31). The Hebrew word translated as *wait* can more literally be translated as *hopeful waiting*.[25] The one who is enduring affliction may not be ready to fly like an eagle or even run without being weary. Suggesting to one who is in the throes of tragedy to fly or run will probably be heard as out of touch and unrealistic, only deepening their feelings of despair, weariness, and isolation. But perhaps with the knowledge of a loving God, one that did not cause their suffering, one that does not use suffering as punishment, and one who exercises power through loving guidance and support, they can begin to emerge from their morass and walk without fainting as they wait hopefully for their strength to be renewed. Christians hold that the spirit of God guides humanity, and it is in our nature to receive this guidance as God delicately honors our freedom. God knows each of our individual situations and is with us as our hopeful waiting progresses in our own unique frame of time. When we are urgently in need of strength and guidance, the gift of God's love will come, showing us a transformed future, even when we least expect or feel we deserve the realization of our hope.

25. Watts, *Word Biblical Commentary*, 95.

11

Plurality: Do Other Faiths Contain Truth?

THE WORLD'S RELIGIONS ARE no longer practiced in isolation. We now live in a diverse religious landscape where persons of different faiths live in close proximity to each other. Although such a multi-religious atmosphere was common at the beginning of Christianity, faith populations gradually became segregated over time. Now, with a return to the former panorama, there is again a heightened awareness of religious plurality and adherents are being pressed about their unique truth claims. Of particular interest are the dialogues between those representing religions which claim to hold *the* singular truth concerning God's relationship to humanity. Christianity, which holds the belief that God is uniquely made known to humanity in Jesus Christ, will be the focus of this chapter. For a Christian, the motivation to explore the diverse religious landscape often begins with the question—"Does our loving God offer salvation to my friend who is a Muslim or Hindu or Buddhist?"

Many discussions among persons of different religions focus on the similarities in the various faiths. I recall a conversation with a lady who was a member of and regularly attended a Christian church. She had recently attended a seminar on world religions and proudly informed me that this event led her to discover she was a Buddhist Christian. I was curious about this revelation and further inquired about this new aspect of her faith. My concerns were eased when I realized it was the emphasis Buddhists place on kindness to all living things that attracted her. I already knew her as a naturalist who takes spiders that have wandered into her house out to the garden instead of exterminating them. And although her own Christian faith also expresses kindness to living things, she had discovered that the concept holds a special place among Buddhists. It is good to find the commonalities between world religions, as they establish an entry point for dialogue. However, the real work of respecting faiths outside of our own comes in discussions about the unique differences.

Most faiths have their own clear convictions and core beliefs which cannot be intermixed with others, as if serving yourself from a buffet. We cannot gloss over the real differences in these convictions without losing the essence of the faith or the meaning it has for one's life. In Christianity, that difference is Jesus Christ, and more specifically, Jesus Christ as the way to salvation. In considering other religions, this belief is the uniqueness that must be addressed. As seen in chapter 5, there are many aspects to salvation and Christians can emphasize these features differently. They may accentuate salvation's restorative forgiveness and healing, or its impact on eternal life, or the transformation of lives which guides them to contribute to bringing peace and justice to earth. But whatever the emphasis, salvation is broadly and unanimously understood by Christians as God's activity through Jesus Christ to bring individuals and all the world to God's intended goal.

Three Approaches

There are three basic frameworks in which Christians currently wrestle with the uniqueness of their faith. The approaches at the furthest and most contrasting ends are labeled *pluralism* and *particularism*. The third and more moderate approach is referred to as *inclusivism*. Classic religious *pluralism* is the belief that two or more religions are equally valid. Pluralists view the various religions as simply different views of God, each with their own saving value, none more true than another.[1] *Particularism*, which has also been referred to as *exclusivism*, makes the case that salvation is only possible through belief and confession in Jesus Christ as savior.[2] Particularists generally emphasize missional evangelism, for they believe salvation is not possible for those of other religions. *Inclusivists* believe that salvation, although only made possible through Jesus Christ, can be experienced by some who have responded to a revelation made available to them by God.[3] For inclusivists, it is by God's grace that non-Christians can experience the salvation

---

1. Grenz et al., *Pocket Dictionary of Theological Terms*, 92.

2. Grenz et al., *Pocket Dictionary of Theological Terms*, 49.

3. Grenz et al., *Pocket Dictionary of Theological Terms*, 65.

brought to the world by Christ. As with all human attempts to explain God's divine workings, there is much to examine in these approaches.

Pluralism

There is no doubt that much religious intolerance and fanaticism has arisen from a conviction that one's faith is the one and only true faith. A pluralist's approach tempers this source of strife by dismissing the idea that any one faith holds the absolute or only truth. It softens differences by expressing, "I have my beliefs and you have your beliefs and they can both be true." The elimination of conflict is gained from this approach, but much is also lost.

To view all religions as equally true and valid is especially attractive to Christians who fear their faith claims and evangelistic efforts promote intolerance through an attitude of dogmatism. But in proposing that all paths are equally true, the possibility that a unique truth exists at all has been sacrificed. This approach, putting all religions on equal footing, surrenders not only the unique salvation beliefs of Christianity but the convicted belief systems of the faithful of any religion.

As a Christian, I can agree that a Muslim holds their faith claims to be true *to them*. However, I cannot hold that their claims are true. Islam's holy book recognizes Jesus as a witness to truth but denies the divinity of Jesus as the Son of God and his role in salvation. The two religions' understanding of Jesus' identity are incompatible. I feel certain that Muslims, Buddhists, and people of the Jewish and many other faiths would likewise claim that Christian beliefs concerning Jesus' identity are not compatible with theirs. These religious systems, at their core, are different, and there is value in recognizing these differences. Pluralists, in abandoning unique religious beliefs for an all-embracing attitude, have made attempts at interfaith dialogue hollow for anyone who authentically holds to their convictions. If we come to a true understanding of another's religion, we can better dialogue with them. As we dialogue, we can eliminate stereotypical assumptions that are often filled with misrepresentations and half-truths. This step is the first toward true civility and elimination of conflict.

Pluralists, however, have compromised this first step by glossing over the differences. In particular, the importance Christians place on Jesus' role in salvation has been diminished by claiming equal salvific paths in other religious systems. Pluralism further negates the unique salvation beliefs of Christianity by re-defining salvation. The pluralist loosely defines salvation as a person maturing out of their self-centeredness.[4] However, such

4. Hick et al., *Four Views on Salvation*, 43.

a definition concentrates on a person's own efforts toward realizing moral and ethical behavior. This is a distinctly different prospect than recognizing the role of Jesus Christ in the means toward this maturing behavior. With this altered definition, dialogue makes a turn toward a comfortable discussion of common moral and ethical positions. Pluralists reaching for biblical support of their views stress moralistic passages such as Matthew 7:12a, "In everything do to others as you would have them do to you" or from Romans 13:9b, "Love your neighbor as yourself." These practical, but not unique, aspects of Jesus' message are included in many other religions. For example, what has been termed the Silver Rule in Confucianism similarly states, "Do not do to others what you would not like yourself."[5]

There is no doubt that there are good people maturing out of their self-centeredness everywhere. Christians are in contact with persons, including friends and relatives, whose religious beliefs are different from their own but who have similar value systems. Nevertheless, no one is perfect, and people of all faiths fail the golden rule at some point in our lives. These transgressions are just what makes Christian salvation beliefs so significant and consequential. When Christians fail to *love their neighbor as themselves*, the unique salvation message of the gospel comes into focus.

Christianity offers forgiveness, a return to the fullness of life, a way forward through the grace of God made possible by Jesus Christ. Simply by opening their contrite hearts to the Holy Spirit, which has come into their lives by their believing in the saving work of Jesus Christ, Christians can find their way to experience restored relationships. Faith systems other than Christianity require a person to be healed by their own efforts by performing some specified action or work. The restored Christian is further empowered by God's grace to effectually participate in bringing more of God's kingdom to earth. It is not difficult to observe that an individual who is living the true Christian faith contributes more to God's will on earth than they would have without participating in the saving work of Jesus Christ. It is these personal heart-changing and transformational aspects of salvation through Jesus Christ that pluralists are willing to surrender.

The pluralist's approach is a popular and currently politically correct option because it does not validate the beliefs of any one religion over another. However, the pluralist's view quickly deteriorates into religious relativism, which is inconsistent with Christianity, as well as inconsistent with many other religions. In relativism, religious truths and effectual paths to salvation are all credible and simply dependent on (relative to) a particular individual or culture. The gravity of what is lost in the pluralist's proposition,

---

5. Smith, *The World's Religions*, 172–73.

namely God's forgiveness and restoration through the unique work of Jesus Christ and the guidance of the Holy Spirit to bring about God's will for the world, prompts us to look at other approaches.

Particularism

Particularism, in its strictest sense, maintains that only those who hear the gospel of Jesus Christ and explicitly respond to that message can experience salvation; all others are eternally lost. This view moves us to another extreme. The assertion of exclusion of so much of the world's population from God's saving grace is what drives many away from Christianity and often into the world of pluralism. Particularists see their missionary activity as a blessing to those that they reach and are unfazed by criticisms of dogmatism or an attitude of superiority. They maintain that these caricatures will always be made toward those who make absolute religious truth claims.[6] However, this outlook shuts down dialogue by signaling to the listener, "I'm right, you are wrong, end of discussion." Particularists stifle authentic conversation and are unwilling to consider any likelihood of a concept or interpretation that might crack the door open to include persons who have not yet confessed Jesus Christ as savior. Unfortunately, this scene is often the only view of Christianity that some are exposed to, and it has led to a grim stereotyping of Christians. If we maintain the above particularist's perspective, we discourage people of other views and faiths from engaging with us, losing the opportunity to learn from them, as well as losing the opportunity to be heard.

Particularists point to many passages for biblical support of their position. Most are from reports of the apostles beginning to separate themselves from other faiths in order to make Jesus known to the world. The most familiar passage, seen advertised in many venues today, is John 3:16; "For God so loved the world that he gave his only Son, so that everyone who believes in him may not perish, but have eternal life." John 14:5–6 also speaks of the relationship of believers to Christ: "Thomas said to him, 'Lord, we do not know where you are going. How can we know the way?' Jesus said to him, 'I am the way, and the truth, and the life. No one comes to the Father except through me.'" Acts 1:8 prepares the apostles for their mission of evangelizing the world with these words: "But you will receive power when the Holy Spirit has come upon you; and you will be my witnesses in Jerusalem, in all Judea and Samaria, and to the ends of the earth." And finally, from Matthew 28:19, we hear Jesus send the apostles into the world

---

6. Hick et al., *Four Views on Salvation*, 192–93.

with these words: "Go therefore and make disciples of all nations, baptizing them in the name of the Father and of the Son and of the Holy Spirit." These verses certainly address a desire for Jesus' message of salvation to be spread throughout the world, but they do not address those outside the effective reach of evangelists.

There are increasing numbers of particularists with a modified approach. Although these particularists likewise feel called to take the message of Jesus as Savior to all the world, they admit they do not know one way or another if salvation is possible for those who have not heard or responded to Christ's message.[7] This position is in contrast to the strict particularists who count non-Christians as eternally lost. But our next approach, inclusivism, has an even more hopeful expectation for those outside of Christianity.

Inclusivism

Inclusivists, like particularists, see God's salvation as only through the work of Jesus Christ. However, they appreciate that God is able to do much more than we can imagine and believe that God's work through Jesus Christ has opened the door for *everyone* and very likely includes a door for persons of other religious persuasions.[8] This perspective differs from particularists in that particularists do not maintain that anyone can be saved outside of a person's specific belief in and declaration of Jesus as Savior, while it differs from pluralists in that pluralists believe all religious systems offer a path to salvation, including those that exclude the path paved by Jesus Christ. For inclusivists, the way to salvation was opened by Jesus Christ, but no claim is made of having a complete grasp of how God directs each person to find and go through that door. Inclusivism auspiciously creates an opening for universal dialogue by admitting a lack of complete understanding of how God brings everyone into the way of salvation through Christ, but at the same time continues to maintain belief in Christ as the way to salvation. Being convicted of one's beliefs yet still being teachable is a very attractive combination. This shift is a refreshing one from the historical inflexibility held by particularists.

The gold standard for testing Christian beliefs is weighing them alongside scripture. The biblical support for particularism is compelling, but the inclusivists take a more comprehensive approach to scripture. While the particularists cling to specific verses in the New Testament, inclusivists focus on God's expansive activity throughout time. Beginning with Genesis,

7. Hick et al., *Four Views on Salvation*, 20.

8. Pinnock, *Wideness in God's Mercy*, 15.

God shows unlimited concern for humanity. God forms covenants to ensure a continuous stream of witnesses to the revelation of God's activity in our lives. The following summarizes the beginning of this unbroken parade of witnesses.

> He [God] is mindful of his covenant forever, of the word that he commanded, for a thousand generations, the covenant that he made with Abraham, his sworn promise to Isaac, which he confirmed to Jacob as a statute, to Israel as an everlasting covenant. (Ps 105:8–10)

Prior to Jesus' earthly ministry, Israel was the nation chosen to be God's witnesses to the world's entire population, but this did not limit God's saving nature to only the Israelite people. God reached the hearts of those outside of Israel as well. There is evidence that no one is beyond the reach of God's voice. God's interactions with pagan believers such as Melchizedek (Gen 14:17–24) and Abimelech (Gen 20:1–18) make it clear that no one is beyond the range of God's sight and mercy. We also see an example of this when God influenced pagan King Cyrus to clear a path for the Israelites to return and rebuild their temple (Ezra 1:1–4). God's ability to call unlikely representatives to speak prophetically for God exists throughout scripture. Amos provides another example.

> Then Amos answered Amaziah, "I am no prophet, nor a prophet's son; but I am a herdsman, and a dresser of sycamore trees, and the Lord took me from following the flock, and the Lord said to me, 'Go, prophesy to my people Israel.'" (Amos 7:14–15)

The Psalmists often express and celebrate that God is present with *all* creation as we can observe in the following verses:

> The Lord is gracious and merciful, slow to anger and abounding in steadfast love. The Lord is good to all, and his compassion is over all that he has made. (Ps 145:8–9)

God's *all*-encompassing compassion and love continue with the arrival of Jesus. Consider this New Testament passage:

> And he [Jesus] is the atoning sacrifice for our sins, and not for ours only but also for the sins of the whole world. (1 John 2:2)

We can also include those passages I previously referenced in support of particularists, for they also witness to God's universal love, God's desire that no one perishes, and that God has established a path to salvation.

In the Old Testament we see God's concern and involvement with those both inside and outside of Israel. And in the New Testament we see Jesus and his disciples continue to witness to God's grace, carrying the message inside and outside of the newly formed Christian circles. There is no reason to think God operates any differently today. The universalism of God's love and ability to stir the human heart is pervasive throughout the Bible, including God's ability to interact with people of all religious persuasions. So, we can have legitimate hope that anyone anywhere can experience the saving grace provided by Jesus. This inclusive nature of salvation is ascertained from scripture, and even though we cannot explain how God's grace works, we can expect God to be drawing all of humanity to Christ's path of salvation.

Summary

Returning to the original question, *is there truth in other world religions?* Yes, we have already seen that there are truths we hold in common with other religions. This realization is where sincere dialogue begins, while the anticipation of finding additional awareness in other religions is where dialogue continues. It is often surprising whom God chooses to use to bring us momentous insights. Do Christians need to relinquish their own beliefs to do this? No. Neither should they expect others to relinquish their beliefs. Listening without an agenda of conversion, allowing the discussion to branch out unbounded, can lead to a lasting and deep civility among those of various religions. That civility, resulting in an elimination of conflict and a growth in love for one another, is the goal. It is through an understanding of one's own faith followed by an open dialogue to reach an understanding of the other's faith that we will see progress in building a global community.

This aspiration is particularly challenging for Christians and Muslims, who both feel directed by God to spread their faith throughout the world. Enriching encounters between these two faiths have been further complicated by historic struggles to gain military, political, and economic power over the limited resources of the world. For many generations, the populations holding to these two religions were relatively isolated from each other. This segregation allowed a breeding ground of misrepresentations and negative attitudes to develop. With the globalization of the world's economy and easy travel, people of both faiths have now been placed in closer proximity. It is time to enter an era of actively trying to understand and accept each other for who we are.

While reading the description of the three positions Christians have made use of to approach other faiths—pluralism, particularism, and inclusivism—it may have occurred to you that the need for dialogue is not limited to persons of different faiths. Persons within a single religion can also benefit from listening to each other. It is important to understand the champions of each of the three frameworks, for they have given us means to address the difficult subject of relating to the world's religions. While we know something is amiss in the relationships between persons of other faiths and recognize the symptoms, the ability to speak heart-to-heart can sometimes elude us. The authors and promoters of these three different views assist us in finding a road map to navigate unfamiliar territory.

We must honestly acknowledge that no one has complete knowledge on this side of eternity. Aware that there is no cookie-cutter solution to the ills in our pluralistic society, we look for ways to sensitively share our faith in the hope that this will create, at the very least, fragile but blooming relationships. We can be pleasantly surprised by insights we encounter from God's use of both Christians and non-Christians in our midst. We must also recognize that our diverse views are often linked to the varied but limited life experiences of each of us. I am sure that my history of receiving God's grace at unexpected times in my life along with living for more than two years in a Muslim country have influenced my outlook. When our experiences raise questions within us, we live without closure, and questions remain. As long as we continue to listen, there is potential to gain new insights; sometimes the best we can do is to live with the questions for a while as we anticipate the possibility of growth. We don't want to lose the value of the question by rushing to a superficial answer.

There is no denying that more work is needed for persons of different faiths to fully live together in peace. But any way forward that is devoid of hope is certainly incomplete. I consider the most hopeful outlook of the three presented views to be inclusivism. It is consistent with Christian beliefs, provides hope for all of creation, and places that hope in God's gracious hands. If we of limited human love desire God's saving grace upon all persons, a desire which is embraced by the champions of all three frameworks, surely God does. Clark Pinnock, a promoter of inclusivism, summarized his vision with the title of his book, *A Wideness in God's Mercy*.[9] Let the grace of God, who loves us *and our neighbor*, prevail.

9. Pinnock, *Wideness in God's Mercy*.

12

Community: Is This the Ultimate Goal?

WHAT IS COMMUNITY AND how is it achieved? Does society overvalue independence and self-sufficiency? Have you ever wished the world was more united? Have you ever longed for more community in your life? Do you ever feel alone and long for assurance that you belong? From the very beginning God made it clear that we are meant to be in the company of others.

> It is not good that the man should be alone. (from Gen 2:18)

A common hindrance to community is our culture's attraction to independence. In such an atmosphere we can find it hard to ask for help, thus missing opportunities to interact with others. This attitude can even carry over into our altruistic endeavors, when our independence causes us to keep our distance when we are helping others. We may find ourselves doing things for others but not with them, thus impeding any sense of partnership. We feel good about the service offered, but in our efficiency, we have missed the opportunity to welcome the other person into our life. The ways which we hinder community can be subtle.

As many have attested, one can be in a room full of people and feel alone, or one can be totally alone and still have a sense of connectedness and belonging. These opposite impressions are possible because community is not solely measured in numbers; it is about a way of life, a way of the heart that leads to sharing our lives with others. We often equate community building with gathering people together, which is certainly a start. In many churches a time is set apart for fellowship after a worship service or a potluck meal is organized in attempts to establish community. However, structured events such as these are no guarantee that community will develop. Community is more than being together, serving together, or working together. Gathering people together for fellowship and establishing community are not the same thing. It takes time, courage, and trust to develop true community.

There are palpable ways we jeopardize community, such as taking offense, stewing in jealousy, or having a conflict of interest. It is hard to feel a sense of belonging when we hold ill feelings toward another. These situations are where the work of restorative forgiveness becomes important. Being able to both offer and accept forgiveness is necessary to maintain community. However, our mobile society makes possible the undemanding option of simply walking away, allowing broken relationships to incumber our hearts. Community takes shape in the heart, and our failures interfere with the process. Just as the work of Christ healed and restored our relationship with God, we are to forgive and restore relationships with each other so that true community can develop.

> Bear with one another and, if anyone has a complaint against another, forgive each other; just as the Lord has forgiven you, so you also must forgive. (Col 3:13)

But perhaps the biggest hindrance to community is an inability to trust another person. Building community does involve risk. We take a risk every time we welcome someone into our lives. We risk having our trust betrayed, and we risk rejection. The fears associated with that risk are only overcome by a series of confidence-building exchanges. While community is in early stages of developing, we must be open and honest about ourselves and the other person. Our expectations need to be reasonable, and we must be careful to not project our own fears, insecurities, and self-doubt on another. Anything that chips away at trust chips away at community. Likewise, anything that welcomes another person into our lives builds community. We can pray for discernment as we consider the risks and begin to seek the trust of another person. And we can make every effort to be that trustworthy friend because sharing our lives with others, building community, is a virtuous and joyful way of life.

Throughout the scriptures we observe that humanity was made with the purpose and predisposition for community. We are not made to champion individualism.

> Bear one another's burdens. (Gal 6:2a)

> If one member suffers, all suffer together . . . if one member is honored, all rejoice together (from 1 Cor 12:26)

> Love your neighbor as yourself. (from Matt 22:39)

We are certainly not made for hostility toward each other.

> Put away from you all bitterness and wrath and anger and wran-
> gling and slander, together with all malice, and be kind to one
> another, tenderhearted, forgiving one another, as God in Christ
> has forgiven you. (Eph 4:31–32)

The bottom line is that God's kingdom embraces a desire for us to live in harmonious community.

> How very good and pleasant it is when kindred live together in
> unity! (Ps 133:1)

Bringing the kingdom of God to earth involves uniting humanity, all of humanity, into one benevolent community. Complete community can be elusive, but nevertheless we are asked to be participants in the endeavor to bring this aspect of God's kingdom to earth. Participating in the endeavor toward creating community gives glory to God and hope to humanity.

The distinct way of life that brings God's kingdom to earth is found in the healing of relationships made possible by Jesus Christ and the power of the Holy Spirit. We have been equipped to participate in this lifestyle. However, when we look further back into the Old Testament, we find that developing community among *all* of humanity has always been crucial to God's plans for us. In the Old Testament the prophet Jeremiah sends a letter to God's people who have been exiled in the foreign land of Babylon. He warned them that their exile would last seventy years. In the meantime, they were to make their homes there and pray for the welfare of those in this alien land whom they now lived among. The community that God desires is not solely among those who know God, but among all people, and he gave instruction on how this could happen.

> But seek the welfare of the city where I have sent you into exile,
> and pray to the Lord on its behalf, for in its welfare you will find
> your welfare. (Jer 29:7)

The wellbeing of the entirety of humanity is God's concern, and God wants it to be our concern as well. As we contribute toward building universal community a sphere of the kingdom of God appears *on earth as it is in heaven.*

The Gospel of Matthew records numerous parables concerning the kingdom of God and how it manifests on earth. Matthew chose the phrase "the kingdom of *heaven,*" which is synonymous with "the kingdom of *God*" in the other gospels. In staying with the tradition of his day, Matthew used the word *heaven* to avoid using the holy name, *God.* It would be easy to skim over the following six parables, thinking they only apply to the heavenly aspects of life, and lose sight of the fact that they relate to building community into our everyday lives here on earth.

> He put before them another parable: "The kingdom of heaven is like a mustard seed that someone took and sowed in his field; it is the smallest of all the seeds, but when it has grown it is the greatest of shrubs and becomes a tree, so that the birds of the air come and make nests in its branches." (Matt 13:31–32)

> He told them another parable; "The kingdom of heaven is like yeast that a woman took and mixed in with three measures of flour until all of it was leavened." (Matt 13:33)

> "The kingdom of heaven is like treasure hidden in a field, which someone found and hid; then in his joy he goes and sells all that he has and buys that field." (Matt 13:44)

> "Again, the kingdom of heaven is like a merchant in search of fine pearls; on finding one pearl of great value, he went and sold all that he had and bought it." (Matt 13:45)

> "Again, the kingdom of heaven is like a net that was thrown into the sea and caught fish of every kind; when it was full, they drew it ashore, sat down, and put the good into baskets but threw out the bad." (Matt 13:47–48)

> "Have you understood all this?" They answered, "Yes." And he said to them, "Therefore every scribe who has been trained for the kingdom of heaven is like the master of a household who brings out of his treasure what is new and what is old." (Matt 13:51–52)

These six parables revealed by Jesus hold powerful insight into the reality of God's kingdom. The kingdom is a tiny seed for now, but it will grow. The grain of yeast is small, but it will slowly raise the bread. The treasure is at present hidden to many, but some will find it and know its worth and joy. And the parable of the net tells us that God's net will reach everyone, but you choose whether or not to participate in his kingdom. And the last of these parables tells us that those who are trained in the way of the Lord, the scribes, spread this new kingdom throughout the world.

The kingdom is truly here now, at least in part; it will grow as long as we let God guide us in doing our part, and then one day it will be complete. It is as if Jesus was holding a diamond up to the light and describing the brilliance of every facet. Although the kingdom of God on earth is, for now, a diamond in the rough, glimpses of it catch our eye, inspiring us to let more and more of its brilliance shine.

Two of the parables (the mustard seed and the yeast) deal with the growth of the kingdom. Three parables (the treasure in the field, the pearl of great price, and the net) describe the joy of finding that there is nothing else as wonderful as the kingdom, and anyone can choose to participate. And one parable (the scribe) defines our role in bringing the kingdom to earth. Sometimes we want miraculous, undeniable proof that the kingdom of God is among us. However, we may only be treated to mere glimpses in the midst of our daily routines. We wait patiently for full fruition, just as we wait for the mustard to grow or the dough to rise. But we participate as we wait.

Some years ago, I commuted daily from the suburbs of San Francisco into the city on the public rail transportation system known as BART (Bay Area Rapid Transit). One morning I was treated to a kingdom of God moment. It so impressed me that if you know me, you have probably already heard this story. I was taking BART into the city during the morning rush hour. If you have ever been a commuter on these systems, you know there are some unspoken rituals during commute hours. For example, where I boarded at the Lafayette station, you line up single file. But at most of the stations in the city you line up two by two. There are no signs telling you this, it is just something all know and do. Also, during the rush hour there is no talking. Each person is expected to remain in their own little world. This small world only extends a few inches around you and stops just short of reaching the next person.

Commuters conform to the expected. Their predictability and precision are a drill sergeant's dream! On this particular morning at the Lafayette station, a gentleman got out of his single file line, walked up to the edge of the platform, and stood on the yellow rubber tiles. Well, everyone knows that the train doors only stop at the black rubber tiles, and lines only form at the black tiles. This peculiar behavior threatened to shatter the morning routine. By the way, I was observing all this from my well-behaved single file line next to his. People were beginning to take note. At first, they frowned, as if to say; what does this man think he is doing? Does he not know the way we operate here?

But we soon realized he had moved closer to the tracks to admire a plant growing through a crack in the concrete. At first all I saw was a spindly plant that looked like it could not survive the wind generated by a passing train. A closer look revealed a crown of small yellow flowers clustered together at the top of this plant. It looked as if these flowers might topple the whole plant at any moment. Several other people began to also look at the flower. There were even some smiles. Smiles on the commuter's faces? This was another departure from the expected behavior. This man had brought something new into the old. He had moved us out of our own thoughts and into a shared experience of God's beauty around us. Was this an example of the kingdom of God breaking through?

Our hearts and spirits had been warmed, right there on the cold, windy platform. We smiled and shared a bit of community. But wait, let's not be too fast to name this a kingdom of God moment. Kingdom of God moments are supposed to change those who experience or observe them. The seed is to grow, the yeast is to result in leavened bread. We are to be transformed more and more into the likeness of Christ. Had we allowed this moment to change us? Were we going to let this yeast expand, or would we punch all the air out of the moment and return to our old ways?

As the train approached and this man headed back to his line, the moment of truth arrived. Had anyone been changed? Here was the test. What were we going to do with this man? Would he, this scribe who gave us a glimpse of making the old new, be given his place back in line? Or does he now have to follow the old rules and go to the end of the line, which had grown significantly by now? By going to the end of the line he would definitely be relegated to standing room only. There was no drill sergeant to restore order. No one was forcing us to live out of our newly found admiration of God's creation and sense of community. This scribe was now providing the commuters with a choice. He was even going to cause words to be spoken during the morning rush hour. Well, the lady he had been behind in line simply said "please" and motioned him in front of her, and we all smiled with relief. Not only had order been restored, but a new possibility, a new way of being had replaced our old rules. Yes, it was a kingdom of God moment, and those of us on the platform had been changed by it.

It was a small thing to notice a delicate flower breaking through the concrete landscape and gain a brief sense of community with one another. Here was a facet of the diamond that most of us would have never seen that morning if we had not been led to it by this scribe. A scribe who has been trained for the kingdom of God reveals the treasure of God's wisdom. They live in the old but make it new. We can be the scribes, the ones trained in kingdom living. We can be the ones who can make small mustard seed differences in the world. The kingdom of God is like some unknown individual in some obscure place who at this hour sits with a person in need.

Sometimes we think that persons who seem to bring the kingdom of God to earth in a big way are the only ones who can make a difference. We admire Martin Luther King Jr.'s commitment to nonviolence, which continues to foster the elimination of injustice. Or we think of Mother Teresa's compassion which was so respected that it caused presidents and kings to take note. Her missions continue to relieve the suffering of the less fortunate. Or we may recall the young student at Tiananmen square who stood in front of the tank. His stand continues to symbolically promote freedom and aid in the fight against oppression. Such outcomes are big demonstrations of the kingdom of God breaking in on earth, and they can be compelling.

But these big demonstrations resulted from the culmination of countless small acts that led up to making their big impact possible. We often forget about all those who marched with King, or the many sisters who selflessly served in Mother Teresa's missions, or the tens of thousands that supported the student demonstrations that for years preceded the famous Tiananmen square protest. These were the many small seeds that were planted before the tree grew to maturity. Indeed, many small actions take place and we seldom know where they might lead. Then, at the right time and the right place, the Holy Spirit brings the world to attention and our small kingdom-of-God actions reveal their full significance.

Jesus used these parables to highlight the necessity of the many small actions. Jesus knew that the enormity of God's infinite wisdom and divine will are far beyond our comprehension. When we struggle to see God's power and God's will holding sway, these parables assure us that we are to continue to plant the little seeds and God will grow the tree. We are to mix in a little yeast and God will leaven three measures of flour. The kingdom of God is like a man who risks his place in a long line to draw attention to a speck of God's creation waving from a crack in the concrete, thus bringing joy and community to a bunch of half-conscious commuters. God is always trying to bring us back to the garden of Eden. We are to be the transporters of God's love and God's will, developing community as we go.

After Jesus' kingdom of God parables, he asks his listeners: "Have you understood all this?" Their affirmative answer indicates they are ready to participate in bringing God's kingdom to earth. We are all theologians attempting to understand our place and role in God's kingdom. We engage with the Christian faith through reflection and critical thinking, and we then translate these beliefs into actions. As theologian N. T. Wright so succinctly pointed out, "Understanding without action is sterile; action without understanding is exhausting."[1] Our actions are to promote fellowship and community as they transport God's kingdom of love, grace, and forgiveness into the world. We continue to face many challenges and these parables tell us of the slow nature of the realization of God's full kingdom on earth. But there is hope in God's promise for the future as the Spirit of God restores each one of us to wholeness and the world to harmony. Even now, as we look

1. Wright, *Matthew for Everyone*, 177.

around, we find evidence of God's kingdom already at hand. I close with a
poem that I wrote while living in the Middle East.

Find the love,
the beauty that surrounds us.
For each it has a different face
to admire,
to ponder,
and embrace.
Sometimes it shines out
where all can see.
The mountain,
the sunset,
or the sea.
Sometimes it hides in faintness
behind despair,
the stark,
or cruel.
Look closely now.
Watch!
A glimmer will soon illuminate
in a smile,
a touch,
or tear.
And once again we'll ponder.
The love,
the beauty,
the mystery.
We were made for love.
It's clear!

Appendix
For Further Reflection—by Chapter

Chapter 1—Belief: Does It Make Any Difference?

Dew, James K., Jr., and Mark W. Foreman. *How Do We Know? An Introduction to Epistemology.* Downers Grove: InterVarsity Academic, 2014.

Lewis, C. S. *Surprised by Joy: The Shape of My Early Life.* New York: Harcourt Brace Modern Classic, 1955.

Moreland, J. P., and William Lane Craig. *Philosophical Foundations for a Christian Worldview.* Downers Grove: InterVarsity Academic, 2003.

Chapter 2—Bible: What Are Its Origins and Use?

Bruce, F. F. *The Canon of Scripture.* Downers Grove: InterVarsity Academic, 1988.

Metzger, Bruce M. *The Canon of the New Testament: Its Origin, Development, and Significance.* 1987. Reprint, Oxford: Clarendon, 2009.

Patzia, Arthur G. *The Making of the New Testament: Origin, Collection, Text & Canon.* 2nd ed. Downers Grove: InterVarsity Academic, 2011.

Chapter 3—Doctrine: What Does It Encompass?

Clark, David K., and Robert V. Rakestraw, eds. *Readings in Christian Ethics.* Vol. 1, *Theory and Method.* Grand Rapids: Baker, 2002.

Kelly, J. N. D. *Early Christian Creeds.* 3rd ed. New York: Longman, 1972.

Olson, Roger E., and Adam C. English. *Pocket History of Theology*. Downers Grove: InterVarsity, 2005.

Chapter 4—Denominations: Are There Versions of Christianity?

Dunn, James D. G. *Unity and Diversity in the New Testament: An Inquiry into the Character of Earliest Christianity*. 2nd ed. London: SCM, 1990.

Olson, Roger E., et al. *Handbook of Denominations in the United States*. 14th ed. Nashville: Abingdon, 2018.

Robinson, Anthony B. *What's Theology Got to Do with It? Convictions, Vitality, and the Church*. Herndon: Alban Institute, 2006.

Chapter 5—Salvation: Can It Be Defined?

Augsburger, David W. *Helping People Forgive*. Louisville: Westminster John Knox, 1996.

Boyd, Gregory, et al. *The Nature of Atonement: Four Views*. Downers Grove: InterVarsity Academic, 2006.

Pinnock, Clark H., and Robert C. Brow. *Unbounded Love*. 1994. Reprint, Eugene, OR: Wipf and Stock, 2000.

Smedes, Lewis B. *The Art of Forgiving: When You Need to Forgive and Don't Know How*. New York: Ballantine, 1996.

Wright, N. T. *Surprised by Hope: Rethinking Heaven, the Resurrection, and the Mission of the Church*. New York: HarperOne, 2008.

Chapter 6—Church: What Function Does It Serve?

Anderson, Ray. *An Emergent Theology for Emerging Churches*. Downers Grove: InterVarsity, 2006.

Green, Gene, et al., eds. *The Church from Every Tribe and Tongue: Ecclesiology in the Majority World*. Carlisle, UK: Langham Global Library, 2018.

Kärkkäinen, Veli-Matti. *An Introduction to Ecclesiology: Ecumenical, Historical & Global Perspectives*. Downers Grove: InterVarsity Academic, 2002.

Patzia, Arthur G. *The Emergence of the Church: Context, Growth, Leadership & Worship*. Downers Grove: InterVarsity, 2001.

Chapter 7—Worship: What Is Its Meaning and Purpose?

Martin, Ralph P. *Worship in the Early Church*. 1974. Reprint, Grand Rapids: Eerdmans, 1998.

Peterson, David. *Engaging with God: A Biblical Theology of Worship*. Downers Grove: InterVarsity, 1992.

Webber, Robert E. *Worship Old and New: A Biblical, Historical, and Practical Introduction*. Rev. ed. Grand Rapids: Zondervan, 1994.

Wright, N. T. *For All God's Worth: True Worship and the Calling of the Church*. Grand Rapids: Eerdmans, 1997.

Chapter 8—Doubt: Can Faith Coexist with Doubt?

Dew, James K., Jr., and Mark W. Foreman. *How Do We Know? An Introduction to Epistemology*. Downers Grove: InterVarsity Academic, 2014.

Moreland, J. P., and Klaus Issler. *In Search of a Confident Faith: Overcoming Barriers to Trusting in God*. Downers Grove: InterVarsity, 2008.

Young, Ben. *Room for Doubt: How Uncertainty Can Deepen Your Faith*. Colorado Springs: David C Cook, 2017.

Chapter 9—Prayer: Does It Change Anything?

Foster, Richard J. *Prayer: Finding the Heart's True Home*. San Francisco: HarperSanFrancisco, 1992.

Hansen, Gary Neal. *Kneeling with Giants: Learning to Pray with History's Best Teachers*. Downers Grove: InterVarsity, 2012.

Chapter 10—Suffering: Why Does God Allow It?

Kushner, Harold S. *When Bad Things Happen to Good People*. New York: Avon, 1981.

Long, Thomas G. *What Shall We Say? Evil, Suffering, and the Crisis of Faith*. Grand Rapids: Eerdmans, 2011.

Weatherhead, Leslie D. *The Will of God*. Nashville: Abingdon, 1972.

Wright, N. T. *Evil and the Justice of God*. Downers Grove: InterVarsity, 2006.

Chapter 11—Plurality: Do Other Faiths Contain Truth?

Hick, John, et al. *Four Views on Salvation in a Pluralistic World*. Grand Rapids: Zondervan, 1996.

Mouw, Richard J. *Uncommon Decency: Christian Civility in an Uncivil World*. Rev. ed. Downers Grove: InterVarsity, 2010.

Pinnock, Clark H. *A Wideness in God's Mercy: The Finality of Jesus Christ in a World of Religions*. Grand Rapids: Zondervan, 1992.

Speight, R. Marston. *God is One: The Way of Islam*. 1989. Reprint, New York: Friendship, 1993.

Chapter 12—Community: Is This the Ultimate Goal?

Grenz, Stanley J., and Jay T. Smith. *Created for Community: Connecting Christian Belief with Christian Living*. Grand Rapids: Baker Academic, 2014.

Willard, Dallas. *Renovation of the Heart: Putting on the Character of Christ*. Colorado Springs: NavPress, 2002.

Bibliography

Adams, Marilyn McCord. *Horrendous Evils and the Goodness of God*. Ithaca, NY: Cornell University Press, 1999.

Aland, Barbara, et al., eds. *Nestle-Aland Novum Testamentum Graece*. 28th ed. Stuttgart: Deutsche Bibelgesellschaft, 2012.

Augustine. *City of God*. Translated by Gerald G. Walsh et al. Garden City, NY: Doubleday, 1958.

————. *Confessions*. Translated by R. S. Pine-Coffin. London: Penguin, 1961.

Balz, Horst, and Gerhard Schneider, eds. *Exegetical Dictionary of the New Testament, Vol. 1*. Grand Rapids: Eerdmans, 1990.

Bishops' Bible. 1568. Edited by Bradford Taliaferro. Reprint, Bible Reader's Museum, 2006.

Brown, Raymond E. *The Churches the Apostles Left Behind*. New York: Paulist, 1984.

Bruce, F. F. *The Canon of Scripture*. Downers Grove: InterVarsity Academic, 1988.

Burns, John, ed. "Belief about or Belief in?" *The Newsletter Newsletter* 28, no. 3 (2006) 6.

Clark, David K., and Robert V. Rakestraw, eds. *Readings in Christian Ethics*. Vol. 1, *Theory and Method*. Grand Rapids: Baker, 2002.

Couper, Heather, and Nigel Henbest. *The History of Astronomy*. Buffalo: Firefly, 2009.

Cross, Frank L., and Elizabeth A. Livingstone, eds. *The Oxford Dictionary of the Christian Church*. Oxford: Oxford University Press, 1997.

Cwiekowski, Frederick J. *The Beginnings of the Church*. New York: Paulist, 1988.

Durham, John I. *Word Biblical Commentary*. Vol. 3, *Exodus*. Waco: Word, 1987.

Goldingay, John. *A Reader's Guide to the Bible*. Downers Grove: InterVarsity Academic, 2017.

Grenz, Stanley J., and Roger E. Olson. *Who Needs Theology? An Invitation to the Study of God*. Downers Grove: InterVarsity, 1996.

Grenz, Stanley, et al. *Pocket Dictionary of Theological Terms*. Downers Grove: InterVarsity, 1999.

Hägglund, Bengt. *History of Theology*. Translated by Gene J. Lund. St. Louis: Concordia, 1968.

Hagner, Donald A. *Word Biblical Commentary*. Vol. 33A, *Matthew 1–13*. of Columbia: Thomas Nelson, 1993.

Heitzenrater, Richard P. *Mirror and Memory: Reflections on Early Methodism*. Nashville: Kingswood, 1989.

Hick, John. *Philosophy of Religion*. Englewood Cliffs, NJ: Prentice-Hall, 1963.

Hick, John, et al. *Four Views on Salvation in a Pluralistic World*. Grand Rapids: Zondervan, 1996.

Hinson, E. Glenn ed. and trans. *Understandings of the Church*. Philadelphia: Fortress, 1986.

Kärkkäinen, Veli-Matti. *An Introduction to Ecclesiology: Ecumenical, Historical & Global Perspectives*. Downers Grove: InterVarsity Academic, 2002.

Kelly, J. N. D. *Early Christian Creeds*. 3rd ed. New York: Longman, 1972.

Kropf, Richard W. *Evil and Evolution: A Theodicy*. Eugene, OR: Wipf and Stock, 2004.

Kushner, Harold S. *When Bad Things Happen to Good People*. New York: Avon, 1981.

Latourette, Kenneth Scott. *A History of Christianity*. Vol. 1, *Beginnings to 1500*. Rev. ed. San Francisco: HarperSanFrancisco, 1975.

Lewis, C. S. *The Problem of Pain*. New York: Macmillan, 1962.

Longenecker, Richard N. "Four Ways of Using the New Testament." In *Readings in Christian Ethics* 1. edited by David K. Clark and Robert V. Rakestraw, 1:185–91. Grand Rapids: Baker, 2002.

Maddox, Randy L. *Responsible Grace: John Wesley's Practical Theology*. Nashville: Kingswood, 1994.

McGiffert, Arthur Cushman. *The Apostles' Creed*. 1902. Reprint, Charleston: Bibliolife, 2019.

Metzger, Bruce M. *The Canon of the New Testament: Its Origin, Development, and Significance*. 1987. Reprint, Oxford: Clarendon, 2009.

———. "To the Reader." In *The New Oxford Annotated Bible: With the Apocryphal/ Deuterocanonical Books*. Edited by Bruce M. Metzger and Roland R. Murphy, ix–xiv. New York: Oxford University Press, 1994.

Metzger, Bruce M., and Roland E. Murphy, eds. *The New Oxford Annotated Bible: With the Apocryphal/Deuterocanonical Books, New Revised Standard Version*. New York: Oxford University Press, 1994.

Milavec, Aaron. *The Didache: Text, Translation, Analysis, and Commentary*. Collegeville, MN: Liturgical, 2003.

Moreland, J. P., and Klaus Issler. *In Search of a Confident Faith: Overcoming Barriers to Trusting in God*. Downers Grove: InterVarsity, 2008.

Moreland, J. P., and William Lane Craig. *Philosophical Foundations for a Christian Worldview*. Downers Grove: InterVarsity Academic, 2003.

Olson, Harriett Jane, et al., eds. *The Book of Discipline of the United Methodist Church*. Nashville: United Methodist, 2000.

Olson, Roger E., and Adam C. English. *Pocket History of Theology*. Downers Grove: InterVarsity, 2005.

Olson, Roger E., et al. *Handbook of Denominations in the United States*. 14th ed. Nashville: Abingdon, 2018.

Outler, Albert C., ed. *John Wesley*. New York: Oxford University Press, 1980.

Packard, Josh, and Ashleigh Hope. *Church Refugees: Sociologists Reveal Why People Are Done with Church but Not Their Faith*. Loveland, CO: Group, 2015.

Patzia, Arthur G. *The Emergence of the Church: Content, Growth, Leadership & Worship*. Downers Grove: InterVarsity, 2001.

Patzia, Arthur G., and Anthony J. Petrotta. *Pocket Dictionary of Biblical Studies*. Downers Grove: InterVarsity, 2002.

Pinnock, Clark H. *A Wideness in God's Mercy: The Finality of Jesus Christ in a World of Religions*. Grand Rapids: Zondervan, 1992.

Roberts, Alexander, and James Donaldson, eds. *Saint Irenaeus of Lyons: Against Heresies*. Rev. ed., 2nd printing. Ex Fontibus, 2015.

Robinson, Anthony B. *What's Theology Got to Do with It? Convictions, Vitality, and the Church*. Herndon, VA: Alban Institute, 2006.

Schaller, Lyle E. *Discontinuity and Hope*. Nashville: Abingdon, 1999.

Schweizer, Eduard. *Church Order in the New Testament*. 1961. Reprint, Eugene, OR: Wipf and Stock, 2006.

Smedes, Lewis B. *The Art of Forgiving: When You Need to Forgive and Don't Know How*. New York: Ballantine, 1996.

Smith, Huston. *The World's Religions*. New York: HarperOne, 1991.

Stanton, Graham N. *The Gospels and Jesus*. Oxford: Oxford University Press, 1989.

Swinburne, Richard. *The Existence of God*. Oxford: Clarendon, 2004.

Watts, John D. W. *Word Biblical Commentary*. Vol. 25, *Isaiah 34–66*. Waco: Word, 1987.

Weatherhead, Leslie D. *The Will of God*. Nashville: Abingdon, 1972.

Wesley, John. *The Complete Sermons*. Lexington, KY: n.p., 2019.

Whitney, Barry L. *What Are They Saying about God and Evil?* New York: Paulist, 1989.

Wright, N. T. *Jesus and the Victory of God*. Christian Origins and the Question of God 2. Minneapolis: Fortress, 1996.

———. *John for Everyone: Part 2*. Enlarged print ed. Louisville: Westminster John Knox, 2015.

———. *Matthew for Everyone: Part 1*. Enlarged print ed. Louisville: Westminster John Knox, 2015.

———. *Paul for Everyone: The Prison Letters*. Enlarged print ed. Louisville: Westminster John Knox, 2015.

Young, Ben. *Room for Doubt: How Uncertainty Can Deepen Your Faith*. Colorado Springs: David C Cook, 2017.